SCOTTISH
REGIONAL
RECIPES

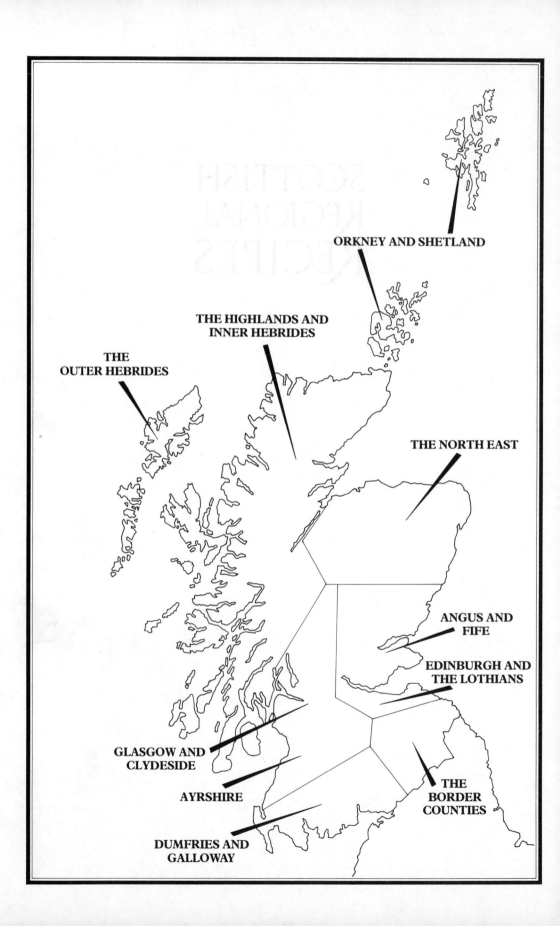

SCOTTISH REGIONAL RECIPES

ORKNEY AND SHETLAND

THE HIGHLANDS AND
INNER HEBRIDES

THE
OUTER HEBRIDES

THE NORTH EAST

ANGUS AND
FIFE

EDINBURGH AND
THE LOTHIANS

GLASGOW AND
CLYDESIDE

AYRSHIRE

THE
BORDER
COUNTIES

DUMFRIES AND
GALLOWAY

SCOTTISH REGIONAL RECIPES

CATHERINE BROWN

Chambers

CHAMBERS
An imprint of Larousse Plc
43–45 Annandale Street
Edinburgh, EH7 4AZ

Published 1992 by W & R Chambers Ltd
Reprinted 1995

First published by the Molendinar Press 1981
Published in Penguin Books 1983

British Library Cataloguing in Publication Data

A catalogue record for this book is available from the British Library

ISBN 0-550-22580-3

ACKNOWLEDGEMENTS
To the people who have freely shared their experiences and
knowledge I would like to say a collective thank you. Talking and
listening to them has provided me with so much help in writing this
book. I am also indebted to many others who have been willing to
taste and criticize the finished results. I am deeply grateful to them all.

C B

Line drawings by Thomas Moulds (p 53)
and Sheila Mackay (pp 20, 58, 109)
Maps by Roy Pearson

Cover design by Art Dept., Edinburgh

Printed by Clays Ltd., St Ives plc

Contents

Introduction

It has always seemed to me that, unless their origins and setting are explained, dishes are meaningless. They tend to run together in the mind, like colours that have run in the wash, so that we are seldom conscious of their individual character. And yet the pattern they make is rich and scintillating.

In Scotland, a varied landscape and extensive coastline has provided the people with many distinctive natural resources which they have used to shape an often unusual and sometimes unique cuisine. It is these dishes, their background and their ramifications, that this book is all about. Like all selections this one reflects my own experiences and tastes, not only by what is included but also by what is left out. No-one can really be impersonal about food, nor can I claim to have included every regional food variation.

Many of my childhood summers were spent on the east coast, rummaging about the beach in front of my grandmother's house for sea-food of all kinds. Whelks and crabs were our favourites. We enjoyed setting out each morning for the hunt, but the eating experience at the end of the day was the greatest thrill of all. We sat for hours picking away meticulously at the shells until the most elusive morsel had been prised out with a pin. It never occurred to us that we might do otherwise than eat them straight from the shells. If we had thought about it, we would probably have rejected the idea – it was the natural flavour which was so crucial to our enjoyment.

The nostalgic food of childhood may or may not have some influence on our later tastes, but I have always liked and looked for the natural taste. In Scotland the larder is lavishly equipped with produce covering a wide range of distinctive natural flavours which the soil, climate, mountain and sea have produced. Simply cooked, they are our greatest asset; as many other countries have discovered who import much of our prime produce.

But this is only one facet of a many-sided subject. As children we had a painful period of adjustment back in Glasgow after our east coast interlude. This was the land of convenience foods for working people – hot pies and bridies from the baker and other hand-held delicacies, often eaten in the streets. My Glasgow grandmother had few facilities in her tiny tenement kitchen and little knowledge of cooking, but somehow or other she knew how to make magnificent broths. Thick and savoury with vegetables and meat, a steaming bowlful was sustaining and satisfying food for hungry children. The ancient Scottish tradition of the permanent pot on the hearth, simmering and stewing over a gentle heat, had survived even in these unlikely circumstances.

Looking at the historical developments in the Scottish diet has its appeal, and much of this book explores the past rather than the future. So why write about an age that is gone?

The age when eight or nine out of every ten Scotsmen scraped a living from a largely hostile land is gone forever – and good riddance to it.

Gradually, as this book evolved, the relevant aspects of the past have emerged. I have tried to be unsentimental about it, always rejecting recipes which were simply not good. In the final analysis culinary excellence will prevail but, obviously, I have included some of the lesser-known indigenous dishes of each area which are not generally eaten or highly regarded in other parts of the country. The poca buidhe and crappit-heads are a Highland experience, linked intimately with the land and sea from which they spring. They are the gift and favour of local people who alone understand them best and these are the sort of dishes which can only be fully appreciated in their local setting. On the other hand, dishes like Orkney clapshot and Shetland whipkull can be made and eaten the world over.

Looking at the map of Scotland, there is a natural divide which cuts slantwise across the country. The Highland fault line, which stretches from about Helensburgh on the west coast up to Stonehaven on the east separates some very different types of country and climate. To the north and west is the rugged high land of plunging mountain torrents and steep-sided fiorded incisions, essentially a land of hill grazings, while the lower land to the east and south is the country of fertile water meadows and rolling cornfields. Within this divide there are many other features of the land, all of which have influenced the history of the inhabitants and have dictated what they have eaten in the past.

The Scots have a deep sense of tradition, national heritage and individualism, which gives us every reason to believe that beneath the uniformity of our mass-produced economy the differences which have been created in the past are unlikely to be substantially changed in the foreseeable future, much less extinguished.

Catherine Brown
Glasgow, 1980

METRIC CONVERSIONS

Since modern packaging now produces commodities like butter, sugar and flour in 250, 500 and 1000 g (1 kg) quantities, and since it is easier anyway to work in proportions of 1 kg, when measuring in metric I have tended to round up the metric measurements making 1 lb = 500 g, ½ lb = 250 g etc. This has been done in all the recipes where a few grams here or there is not going to make any substantial difference to the finished result, except perhaps to produce slightly larger quantities. In order to preserve the liquid balance I have rounded up the liquid volumes. In some recipes, however, there is a delicate balance which cannot be disturbed, particularly in baking, so here I have stayed with the nearest metric equivalent.

Unless otherwise stated, all recipes will serve approximately 4 to 6 people, depending on the size of the portion required.

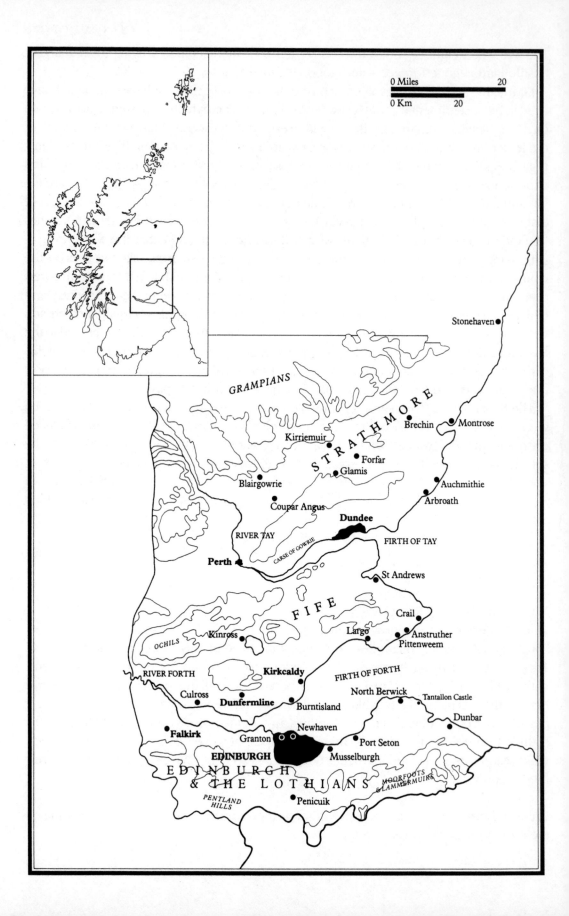

I. *Edinburgh and the Lothians*

THE LOWLANDS

Of all the regions of Scotland the Lowlands has always had the largest area of habitable land. Fertile, workable land, a warmer climate and the three large estuaries of Forth, Clyde and Tay giving greater access to sea transport, have all contributed to the situation that today seventy-five per cent of Scotland's population live and work here on only one-seventh of the country's area.

This area, and especially the great cities of Edinburgh and Glasgow, has always been the receiving and mixing place of the restless, the ambitious and the forcibly uprooted from all the rest of Scotland and beyond. To Glasgow have come dispossessed Highlanders in large numbers, while Edinburgh has seen a similar influx from the Orkneys and Shetlands. But despite this and many other immigrations, the Lowlands has absorbed them and never lost its character. It remains the heart of Scotland and the Lowlander, with his vigour and forthrightness – perhaps with a touch of harshness from his Calvanistic past – remains unpretentious and realistic. The *Lallans* have given their name to the ancient Scottish tongue known also as 'the Doric' or 'Braid Scots'. This is the tongue which Scottish poets and writers have fought to keep alive, and it is still preserved in many of the traditional dishes and cooking terms such as *girdle, bannock, farl, bree, het pint* and *drappit*.

Within the region are several distinctive areas almost as separate in their own way as the Lowlands are from the Highlands. The two largest cities, Edinburgh and Glasgow, have established their own distinctive characteristics; and this is reflected in a natural division between east and west in the produce of the land. In the eastern half of the country there are the districts of Fife, Perthshire, Angus, Kincardine and the Lothians, which all have a drier, colder climate with a little more sunshine than the western areas. Here the soils are more fertile so that generally crops are grown. By contrast, rich pasturelands in the moist western districts are used for grazing large herds of dairy cattle, particularly in Ayrshire.

EDINBURGH AND THE LOTHIANS

Along the south shore of the Firth of Forth lie the three counties which make up the ancient province of Lothian. Dominating the region, as it has throughout history, is Edinburgh. With a productive hinterland, enclosed to the south by the long east-west stretch of uplands known as the Pentland, Moorfoot and Lammermuir Hills, this is one of Scotland's richest agricultural regions. Large areas of fertile lowlands, sunny summers and a dry climate make it a very productive arable farming region.

Musselburgh is the centre of a market-garden belt which stretches along the coast from Edinburgh to North Berwick, often referred to as 'the garden of Scotland'. Almost every sort of vegetable is grown – cabbages, brussels-sprouts, turnips, cauliflowers, peas, lettuce, onions. Musselburgh is particularly famous for its leek crop. Between a half and two-thirds of Scotland's vegetables are grown here for the large urban markets of the rest of Central Scotland. The Edinburgh area has a long history of agricultural enterprise. As early as the 12th and 13th centuries it contained many large gardens and orchards, tended by monks well-versed in fruit husbandry. David I, a skilled horticulturist, was known to have had a large garden at the foot of the Castle rock. In a map of 1647 large gardens appear at the back of houses in the Royal Mile.

By the 18th century there were plenty of 'improvers' in this area who set the agricultural revolution moving throughout the rest of Scotland. Their methods produced high yields of root and grain crops which meant that there was a considerable surplus. Corn and wheat were exported to Spain and Portugal, oats to Ireland, Ayrshire and the Western Highlands.

BAKING AND CONFECTIONERY

Although the Lothians do not have heavy industries on the same scale as Glasgow, milling developed as a direct result of surplus grain. From this emerged a baking, chocolate and confectionery industry which still specialises in many varieties of the traditional shortbreads, oatcakes, bannocks, scones and cookies.

Midlothian Oatcakes

3 oz dripping, lard, margarine or butter (75 g)	4 oz plain flour (125 g)
	1 tsp baking powder
	½ tsp salt
8 oz medium oatmeal (250 g)	Water to mix

Preheat the oven to 300°F/150°C or gas mark 2

Melt fat in a pan. Put flour, oatmeal, baking powder and salt into a bowl. Make a well in the centre and add fat and enough water to make a stiff dough. Roll out and cut

Oatcakes are like shortbread, in that many varieties exist and every housewife has her own favourite. Lowlanders, in general, with a greater variety of grains to choose from, were quite happy to mix grains, as in this recipe, but Highlanders would never dream of using two kinds together. Their oatcakes are always made with

11

oatmeal only, plus a very little fat and water, which makes them quite brittle and delicate, requiring a certain amount of skill in handling. This recipe makes oatcakes that are more pliable and easier to work and they retain a good crispness and flavour. A Highland purist would probably be appalled at such a mixture.

dough. Roll out and cut into rounds about 2½" (6 cm) in diameter. Bake in a warm oven for 30 minutes.

Petticoat Tails

A baking speciality of the area, now made commercially, which takes its name from the shape of the petticoat hoops worn in the nineteenth century. The original recipe in Meg Dods' Cook and Housewife's Manual *included a little milk, which is not used today; otherwise it is simply a good shortbread with an interesting shape. It is a ladies' shortbread, as men usually prefer the thick fingers.*

7 oz plain flour (200 g)	2 oz icing sugar (50 g)
3 oz butter (75 g)	1 dsp caraway seeds
1 oz lard (25 g)	(optional)

Preheat the oven to 350°F/180°C or gas mark 4

Sift the flour and icing sugar into a bowl. Add the butter and lard and rub in fats till the mixture resembles fine breadcrumbs. Add caraway seeds and then turn the mixture out onto a board and knead together into a firm dough.

Roll out into a large round about ¼" (½ cm) thick. Crimp the edges with your finger and thumb. Prick all over with a fork then cut a circle out of the centre. Divide the rest of the circle into either twelve, eighteen or twenty-four pieces, depending on the size you want. Bake on a greased baking sheet for 20–30 minutes or until they are a pale golden brown. Dredge with caster sugar while still hot.

Edinburgh Gingerbread

This rich gingerbread should not be judged by normal cake standards, since it may sink in the middle as it cools and will eat 'heavy'.

6 oz butter or margarine (150 g)	3 tsp bicarbonate of soda
	1 tsp mixed spice
6 oz brown sugar (150 g)	2 tsp powdered ginger
8 oz black treacle (225 g)	3 oz raisins or dates
3 eggs	(75 g)
milk to mix	2 oz flaked almonds or
9 oz flour (250 g)	walnuts (50 g)

Preheat the oven to 350°F/180°C or gas mark 4

Put the butter and sugar into a fairly large pan and warm very slightly, without melting too much, and cream them together. Put the pan onto the scales and measure in the treacle. Warm again slightly and beat in the eggs one at a time. Add the fruit and nuts and then sift in the other dry ingredients. Mix with milk to make a soft-dropping consistency. Pour the mixture into a 7" (18 cm) round cake tin and bake in a moderate oven for about ¾ hr or until it feels springy on top.

Edinburgh Tart

6 oz puff pastry (150 g)
For the filling –
2 oz butter (50 g)
2 oz sugar (50 g)

2 oz chopped candied
    peel (50 g)
1 oz sultanas (25 g)
3 eggs

This was a high tea baking speciality.

Preheat the oven to 450°F/230°C or gas mark 8

Line an 8" (20 cm) flan ring with pastry. Melt the butter very gently in a pan and add sugar, candied peel, sultanas and eggs. Beat together and then pour into the pastry case. Bake in a very hot oven for 15–20 minutes and then serve hot or cold with a bowl of cream.

Edinburgh Rock

1 lb granuated sugar
   (500 g)
7½ fl oz water (200 ml)

Pinch of cream of tartar

The Scottish confectionery industry is probably best known for its Edinburgh Rock. This is not the customary solid stick with letters down the centre but a light, pastel-coloured sugary confection, delicately flavoured, which requires a certain amount of care and dexterity in the making.

Flavouring and colouring:
lemon *(yellow)*, peppermint *(green)*, raspberry *(pink)*, vanilla *(white)*, ginger *(fawn)*, and orange.

Put the sugar and water into a pan and heat, stirring until the sugar dissolves. Just before it boils, add the cream of tartar. Boil till the temperature reaches 250°F/130°C or the sugar forms a hard ball when a little is dropped into some cold water. This is an important point since the sugar will be too sticky to 'pull' if it is not hard enough. If too hard it will not crystallise well. Remove from the heat and add colouring and flavouring. Let it stand for a few minutes to cool slightly, then pour it out onto a buttered marble slab or into buttered confectioner's candy bars (a buttered formica top will also do, provided you have cooled the sugar slightly before pouring out).

It was discovered by accident when Alexander Fergusson, popularly known as 'Sweetie Sandy' came across a piece of confectionery which he had overlooked and left lying untouched for several months. He became one of 19th-century Edinburgh's most successful confectioners and Edinburgh Rock is now exported all over the world.

Turn the edges into the centre as it cools with a buttered scraper. Do not stir. When it is cool enough to handle, dust it well with icing sugar and take it up in your hands. 'Pull' the sugar by letting it drop and then bringing it up again. Do not twist it. Continue this process till it starts to harden up, then pull into one long strip about $\frac{1}{2}''$ (1 cm) thick. Leave to set hard then break into even-sized pieces.

Dust a tray with icing sugar and place the pieces of rock on it. Dust the rock with icing sugar and leave in a warm atmosphere till the rock becomes powdery and soft. The time this takes varies from one to two days up to a week. Store in an airtight tin.

This is a good shortbread variation, despite its misleading name. Tantallon Castle is a ruined stronghold, now a national monument, several miles east of North Berwick.

Tantallon Cakes

8 oz plain flour (225 g)	1 oz caster sugar (25 g)
1 tbsp rice flour	1 tsp grated lemon rind
4 oz butter (100 g)	

Preheat the oven to 325°F/170°C or gas mark 3

Sift the flour into a bowl. Take out one tablespoonful and replace this with one tablespoonful of rice flour.

Now add the sugar and lemon rind. Finally work in the butter with your hands. It may be easier to turn it out onto a board to do this, but it should come together into a lump the consistency of putty.

Place on a floured board and press with your hands, not with a rolling pin, till it is about $\frac{1}{2}''$ (1 cm) thick. Cut into rounds about $1\frac{1}{2}''$ (4 cm) diameter. Place on a greased baking sheet and bake in a cool oven for about 25–30 minutes.

Sprinkle thickly with caster sugar while still hot.

NINETEENTH CENTURY EDINBURGH SPECIALITIES

Early in the nineteenth century Scotland was 'discovered' by the rest of Europe, and Edinburgh people in turn discovered the great advantage of their Scottishness. Being a capital and the point of entry for the aristocratic tourist gave the city a special self-awareness, cosmopolitan in the eyes of the rest of Scotland and Scottish in the eyes of the European romantic. Old Scots dishes and customs which had been formerly thought a little uncouth were taken up again and favoured by the Edinburgh intelligentsia.

The man who had done most to develop and foster this new consciousness was Sir Walter Scott. Not only in his prolific writings but throughout his life he did much to revive a feeling of national identity. One of his better-known acts was to unearth the old Scottish Crown jewels, when no-one seemed quite certain where they had been put, and have them displayed in

Edinburgh Castle. While previously Edinburgh had been the classical, intellectual and artistic city of David Hume, Adam Smith, Raeburn and Dugald Stewart, Scott made it into a popular romantic one of drama, feeling and heroic action.

Scott is said to have encouraged the publication of *The Cook and Housewife's Manual* by Mistress Margaret Dods of the Cleikum Inn, St Ronans in 1826 (see also p. 15). Most of it was actually compiled and written by Mrs Isobel Johnston, wife of an Edinburgh publisher, but the introduction is thought to have been written by Scott. In it, the St Ronan's Culinary Club is formed to preserve and publicise the gastronomic excellencies of Scottish fare.

Cock-a-Leekie

2½–3 lb boiling fowl (1¼–1½ kg)	Salt and pepper
6 pt water (3 L)	1¼ lb leeks, finely chopped (625 g)
2 medium onions, finely chopped	2 oz long grain rice (50 g)
Bay leaf, sprig of thyme and some parsley stalks	

Garnish
Chopped parsley

Put the fowl into a large, deep pot and add water. Bring slowly to the boil then skim and reduce to a gentle simmer. Now add the herbs (tied together), salt and pepper, onions, and the white part of the leeks. Simmer for 1½–2 hours or until the meat is tender. Half-an-hour before the end of cooking add the rice.

Remove the bird and leave to cool slightly. Add the green of the leek and cook for another 10 minutes. When the bird is cool enough, remove some of the flesh and chop up roughly. Return to the soup and heat through. Check seasoning, remove herbs and serve garnished with parsley. Serves 12–14.

Among the recipes for Haggis, Sheep's Head Broth, Hotch Potch and other well-known national specialities which are to be found in the Manual, *Cock-a-leekie is one which seems to have been very popular in Edinburgh at this time. Perhaps the Musselburgh leek tradition had something to do with this; also it was the custom throughout the country to keep poultry. This was not quite so easy in towns, but there are accounts of people managing to keep chickens in their back yards. Often the medieval custom of rent payments in kind were practised and poultry was most popular for this exchange.*

Sometimes the birds were poor specimens, only fit for the boiling pot, but with plenty of flavour, which is perfect for Cock-a-Leekie. Today it is best to use a boiling fowl, which a good fishmonger is more likely to have than a butcher. Prunes were originally added to sweeten the broth, if the leeks were particularly old and bitter, but this is now a matter of taste.

Tweed Kettle

It seems that this was the equivalent in the nineteenth century of our Mince and Tatties today. Salmon was so plentiful that the poor people complained about having to eat so much, and this dish was commonly known as Salmon Hash. It was sold in cook-shops in Edinburgh with mashed potatoes, and the salmon presumably came from the Tweed.

2 lb fresh salmon (1 kg)	2 tbsp shallots or chives,
Salt and pepper	finely chopped
Pinch of mace	2 tbsp parsley or dill,
¼ pt fish stock (125 ml)	finely chopped
¼ pt white wine (125 ml)	1 oz butter (25 g)
¼ lb mushrooms, finely	
chopped (125 g)	

Put the whole piece of fish into a deep pan which just fits it neatly. Cover with water and bring slowly to the boil. Simmer for one minute and remove salmon from the pan. The skin will now peel off easily and the bones should be filleted out. Now cut up the fish into pieces approximately 1" (2.5 cm) square.

Return the skin and bones to the cooking liquor and simmer for 15–20 minutes. Strain. Put ¼ pt (125 ml) of this cooking liquor and the white wine into a pan and add the salmon and shallots. Season with salt, pepper and mace. Cover and simmer for 3–4 minutes. Add parsley or dill and check seasoning.

Melt butter in a pan and add mushrooms. Cook gently till soft and add to the fish. Cooked shrimps or hard-boiled eggs, finely chopped, were sometimes added and it was served hot with creamed potatoes, cold with cress and cucumber.

Stoved Howtowdie

An old Scottish dish which typically uses a pot rather than the oven for roasting chicken. The 19th-century garnish was rounds of spinach topped with poached eggs and grilled bacon, which was known as Howtowdie wi' Drappit Eggs. The word Howtowdie comes from the French Letoudeau ('fat young chicken').

3 lb chicken for roasting	*For the stuffing –*
(1½ kg)	6 oz medium oatmeal
1 oz butter (25 g)	(175 g)
12 button onions	1 medium onion or a
A little grated nutmeg	small leek, finely
A few sprigs of lemon	chopped
thyme	2 oz any kind of fat or suet
¼ pt water or giblet stock	(50 g)
(125 ml)	

Use a heavy, thick-based pot which the chicken will just fit neatly into.

Make up the stuffing first in a frying pan. Melt the fat and add onion or leek. Cook gently to soften, but do not brown. Stir in the oatmeal and season well. Cook for a few minutes, stirring occasionally. Stuff into the body and neck cavities of the chicken. Fold over the neck flap and fix with a skewer.

Melt the butter in the pot and turn the chicken to brown lightly on all sides. Add peeled onions and sprinkle nutmeg and thyme over breast. Add boiling water or stock and fit on lid securely. Cook slowly over a low heat for 1½–2 hours.

To serve, remove chicken from the pot and place on serving ashet. Reduce cooking liquor slightly by boiling for a few minutes, then season. Pour some of the cooking liquor over the chicken and serve the remainder in a sauce boat. Serve with spinach and grilled bacon.

Roast Haunch of Red Deer

3–5 lb haunch of venison (1¼–2½ kg)	Flour for dredging
	For larding –
4 oz melted butter (125 g)	Piece of pork fat
½ pt game stock or water (300 ml)	Larding needle
	For marinade –
1 level tsp mixed spice	1 pt red wine (½ L)
Salt	Juice of 3 lemons

Preheat the oven to 425°F/220°C or gas mark 7

Begin by larding the venison. Make sure the pork fat is very cold. If necessary put in the freezing compartment of the refrigerator for an hour. Cut into strips 2″ long (5 cm) and just over ¹/₈″ wide (½ cm). Thread a strip of fat through a larding needle and then take a small stitch in the joint. Repeat until the whole joint is studded with fat. If you do not have a larding needle, the whole piece of fat can be tied onto the joint. This is best for smaller joints and a good method for a saddle of venison.

The next step is to rub some salt and spice into the meat. Then soak in wine and lemon juice, turning and basting for at least 6 hours – overnight if possible.

Place the joint in the roasting tin, add marinade and pour over melted butter. Cover with some foil or brown paper and put into a very hot over for 10 minutes to brown – then reduce the heat to 350°F/180°C or gas mark 4. Roast for 15 minutes per pound plus 15 minutes. Baste occasionally and turn the meat once. Fifteen minutes before it is ready, remove the foil, baste with pan juices and dredge with flour. Put back into the oven to brown on top.

Remove from the oven and place on a serving ashet in a warm place for 10–15 minutes to allow the meat to set and the juices to settle.

To make up the gravy, pour off some of the surplus fat. Add game stock and reduce. Check seasoning and finish with a little lemon juice. Serve very hot with some Rowan and Apple or Redcurrant Jelly.

Allow 8 oz (225 g) meat on the bone per person.

The royal castle of Holyrood was an obvious source of traditions and customs. This roast venison recipe appeared in the Annals of the Cleikum Club *as one of their most prized possessions. The method is supposed to have been invented by the 'Master of the Kitchen of Mary of Guise and had ever since been preserved a profound secret.'*

Holyrood Pudding

This is a very sophisticated semolina pudding which has an excellent flavour and a light soufflé texture.

2 oz semolina (50 g)	2 oz ratafia biscuits
1 oz butter (25 g)	(50 g)
2 oz sugar (50 g)	2 tbsp marmalade
1 pt milk (500 ml)	3 eggs

Preheat the oven to 350°F/180°C or gas mark 4

Put the milk into a large pan and bring slowly to the boil. Just before it boils sprinkle in the semolina, stirring all the time. Add butter, sugar and marmalade and cook for about five minutes, stirring all the time.

Leave aside to cool a little. Separate the eggs and stir in the yolks. Beat up the whites stiffly. Mix in the ratafias, then gently fold in the whites with a tablespoon. Pour into a greased 3 pt (1½ L) pie dish. Bake in a moderate oven for 20–30 minutes, when it should be nicely risen and brown on top.

Barley Pudding

This was eaten in the Lothians as an accompaniment to meat and other savoury dishes. It has its origins in the ancient dish of frumenty, which was a kind of pudding made of milled wheat, cooked in milk or water and flavoured with spices and dried fruit.

3 oz barley (75 g)	2 oz currants (50 g)
1 pt water (500 ml)	

Preheat the oven to 300°F/150°C or gas mark 2

Wash the barley and put in a 2 pt (1 L) ovenproof dish. Cover with water and bake for 3 hours. Stir in the currants for the last 20 minutes. Serve with sugar and single cream or milk.

CHEESE

Although not a major cheese-producing area on the same scale as the South-West, the Lothians do have a few local creameries. In the village of Penicuik in Midlothian, an enterprising farming family have established a market for some of the traditional Scottish cheeses. The business started on a shoestring, selling home-made cheeses at the farm 'road end' in 1966. Later they opened a farm milk bar and began to produce the Howgate range of cheeses.

This includes **Crowdie**, a soft cheese made from skimmed milk and **Cottage cheese**, which is similar to Crowdie but more bland with less salt. A variety of this is made with garlic, herbs and cream, while another type is the **Peat-Smoked Soft Cheese** which is a full-fat mild cheese. **Oatmeal Cream Cheese** is a double cream cheese rolled in oatmeal. **Goat's Milk Soft Cheese** is also made from the full-fat milk. At one time in Scotland's history goats were more numerous than sheep and their cheese was an important home industry. As in Wales, cheese was also frequently made from ewe's milk, and at the Howgate creamery this is sometimes made if the milk is available.

Buttermilk and soured cream are also available and as a by-product, milk-fed pork is sold here since it is useful to have a consumer for the leftover skimmed milk from the cheese-making process.

FISHING

The south side of the Forth, like the Fife coast, saw the growth of numerous small fishing havens concerned mainly with herring and oyster-fishing. With herring in scarce supply now, and the oyster beds long ago polluted, other fisheries have developed. At Port Seton, Fisherrow, Dunbar and Newhaven some small vessels fish for white fish and shellfish. Distinct from the inshore fisheries is the trawling industry centred on Granton, fishing distant waters for haddock, whiting, cod and herring.

Newhaven Cream

1 lb Aberdeen fillet (500 g)	Salt and pepper
½ pt milk (300 ml)	*For the sauce –*
1½ oz melted butter (40 g)	Milk the fish was cooked in plus:
3 oz fine white bread-crumbs (75 g)	¼ pt additional milk (125 ml)
2 tbsp chopped parsley	½ oz butter (15 g)
3 eggs	½ oz flour (15 g)
¼ pt cream (125 ml)	1 tbsp chopped parsley

This dish was more likely to have been developed in the kitchens of fashionable Edinburgh than in the fisher houses down the hill in Newhaven.

Put the fish into a pan with the milk. Bring to the boil, cover and simmer for 5 minutes. Remove the fish, skin and flake. Put all the other ingredients into a bowl and add the fish. (Do not add the milk the fish was cooked in). Mix together and pour into a greased 2 pt (1 L) soufflé mould. Cover with greaseproof paper or foil and bake in a moderate oven for 30 minutes. Set the dish in a tin with about 1″ (2.5 cm) of water in it. This prevents the egg overcooking. It may also be steamed in a bowl for 1–1½ hours.

To make the sauce – melt the butter in a pan and add the flour. Cook for a few minutes without browning then add the milk gradually. Boil up to thicken, season and add parsley. When the fish is cooked, turn out onto a heated ashet and coat with the sauce. Serve hot.

Musselburgh Pie

1½ lb rump steak (675 g)	1 tbsp seasoned flour
2 medium onions, finely chopped	3 lb fresh mussels (1½ kg)
2 tbsp oil	1½ oz beef suet (40 g)
½ pt water (300 ml)	½ lb puff or rough-puff pastry (25 g)
Salt and pepper	

When oysters were so plentiful that the poor regarded them as basic fare, and cooks threw handfuls of shelled ones into soups and sauces for extra flavour, this pie was popularly made with them wrapped up inside the meat. Although it can be made very successfully with mussels, perhaps one day oysters can be used again if the revival in oyster-farming on the West Highland coast is successful.

Preheat the oven to 350°F/180°C or gas mark 4

Cook the mussels first. Put them in a pan of boiling salted water about 2″ (5 cm) deep, cover with a lid and boil for 2–3 minutes. Remove them from their shells.

Heat the oil in a pan and cook the onions till golden brown. Beat out the steak till it is quite thin and cut into strips. Place a few mussels and a piece of suet on each strip, season and roll up. Dip in seasoned flour and pack into a 2 pt (1 L) pie dish round a pie funnel. Add onions and water, cover with foil and put in a moderate oven to cook for 1½–2 hours or until the meat is tender. Remove from the oven and leave to cool. When cool cover with pastry, trim and decorate. Brush with milk or beaten egg and make some holes in the top for ventilation. To cook the pastry put into a hot oven 425°F/220°C or gas 7 and bake for 30 minutes.

2. Angus and Fife

ANGUS LANDSCAPE

When you pass through Perth and into this northern-most part of the Lowlands, you either go inland and through the wide valley of Strathmore or along the coast and through the narrower strip of land known as the Carse of Gowrie. Whichever your route, it is a land of rich farmlands with solid, square farmhouses, and many castles guarded by old woods and encased in high walls with trees everywhere.

The Angus trees are famous. Beech, ash, rowan, silver birch, and Scots firs, all are rooted in the old red sand-stone soil and act as valuable protection for the farm-lands. This distinctive red soil, free from stones, easy to work and retentive of moisture, attracted Cistercian monks who came to Scotland in the Middle Ages with a religious purpose and also their more advanced farm-ing methods. They began a farming tradition here which grew and developed throughout the centuries so that today, as you pass through it, you can feel a sense of age in this rich sheltered land. It is an old countryside steeped in the past; but not always a peaceful past. The land and the people were easy prey for the marauding Highland clansmen who made their way down the con-venient Angus glens to snatch food and livestock from Lowland lairds.

ABERDEEN ANGUS BEEF

This is the homeland of the pedigree Aberdeen Angus herds of beef cattle which are one of Scotland's most famous exports.

The breed was recognised by the Highland Agricul-tural Society which reported in 1835: 'We cannot but regard it as the most valuable breed of Scotland, com-bining as it does in a great measure the constitution of the Highlander and the feeding properties of the Shorthorn.' It was an amalgam of several breeds which combined to produce the hornless animal of almost uniformly black colour.

Though the Aberdeen Angus looks small in compari-son with other beef cattle, this is because of its short legs and compact, rounded form. In fact, by weight it is classed among the larger breeds. Meat is concentrated on the most valuable parts, while the marked absence of waste throughout the carcass makes it a butcher's favourite. The meat is renowned for its fine flavour and juiciness, which to a large extent is due to the marbled effect of the fat dispersed throughout the meat.

There are few regional recipes documented using this prime quality beef because traditionally stock was always sold for badly-needed capital. It is a well-known fact today that the traditional Roast Beef of Old England was founded on prime Scottish beef. Scots considered themselves lucky if they had some blood to make puddings. Originally the cattle were herded south by drovers from all over Scotland for fattening on the richer lands of Southern England.

Another reason for the lack of traditional recipes is that such excellent meat needs only the simplest methods of cooking. Very little needs to be added and nothing taken away from the natural flavour of the meat.

Roast Aberdeen Angus Beef

3–4 lb Sirloin, Wing, Fore or Middle Rib Roast (1½–2 kg)
2–3 oz dripping or butter (50–75 g)
1 level tbsp powdered mustard
2 tbsp lightly browned flour
Freshly ground black pepper
½–¾ pt water (250–400 ml)

Preheat the oven to 400°F/200°C or gas mark 6

Roasting was not a method of cooking which the Scots indulged in a great deal. Scant supplies of fuel meant that the country generally depended more on the boiling–stewing tradition but it seems appropriate that today we should lay claim to Roast Aberdeen Angus Beef as one of our most prized regional specialities.

Melt the butter or dripping, pour over the meat and spread evenly over the whole surface with your hand. Lightly brown the flour in a pan and mix with the mustard and pepper. Sprinkle this mixture evenly over the meat. Leave at room temperature for about an hour to absorb the flavours.

When ready to roast, put the meat onto a rack over a roasting tin and put into a hot oven for 20–25 minutes to brown the meat. Reduce the heat to 350°F/180°C or gas mark 4 and allow approximately 15–20 minutes per lb if you like the meat rare, 20–25 minutes per lb for medium, 25–30 minutes per lb for well done.

Remove the meat from the oven and season with salt. Place on a heated serving ashet and keep in a warm place for 15–20 minutes before carving. This allows the juices to settle and the meat to set which makes it easier to carve. Meanwhile prepare the gravy by pouring off the surplus fat and leaving the residue. Add water and bring to the boil stirring in the pan residues. Simmer to reduce slightly. Season and strain into a sauceboat to serve with the roast. Serve with roast potatoes and green vegetables.

Allow 6–8 oz (150–225 g) meat on the bone or 6 oz (150 g) without bone per person.

In the vale of Strathmore, Forfar is the largest town and an important centre of the Aberdeen Angus cattle trade. The farmers come to the 'mart' every Monday, and one of the local beef specialities enjoyed here and all over Angus is the Forfar Bridie. Making bridies has always been more of a commercial than a domestic enterprise, with bakers in the town able to look back on three generations of bridie-making. Before this the pies are reputed to have been made for selling at local fairs and markets by Maggie Bridie of Glamis, who almost certainly gave her name to them.

Forfar Bridies

1 lb rump steak or topside (500 g)	*For the pastry –*
	12 oz plain flour (400 g)
3 oz beef suet (75 g)	3 oz margarine (100 g)
2 medium onions, finely chopped	3 oz lard (100 g)
	Water to mix
Salt and ground black pepper to taste	Salt

Preheat the oven to 400°F/200°C or gas mark 6

To make the pastry, rub the fat into the flour, add salt and mix to a very stiff dough with water. Divide into four equal-sized pieces and roll out on a floured board into four large ovals.

Beat out the steak with a meat bat and cut into roughly ½" (1 cm) squares. Chop up suet finely. Put the meat into a bowl with the suet and onions. Add seasonings and mix well. Divide meat into 4 portions and cover half of each oval with meat, leaving a rim for sealing. Wet edges, fold over and seal. Use finger and thumb to crimp edge. Make a hole in the top. Bake on a greased baking sheet in a fairly hot oven for 45 minutes.

The edge of the Grampian Highlands is interrupted at several points by the deep and very beautiful Angus glens descending to Strathmore. Their valleys are dotted by scattered and remote farms, set in ploughlands and pasture with sheep grazing on the steep slopes of the glens. Beyond this, on the higher moorlands, are the shooting estates with rich supplies of game. Some of this finds its way into the lowland areas where this pie is made, combining game with the local beef.

Lowland Game Pie

For the stock –	½ lb rump steak (250 g)
Bones and carcasses from birds	1½ oz butter (40 g)
1 onion, finely sliced	3 oz streaky bacon, diced (75 g)
1 carrot, diced	1 medium onion, finely chopped
1 bay leaf	
2 pt water (1 L)	1 oz flour (25 g)
For the marinade –	Salt and pepper
½ pt red wine (¼ L)	Beaten egg for brushing
2 tbsp olive oil	8 oz puff pastry (250 g)
For making up the pie –	
1 lb meat from the birds (500 g)	

Preheat the oven to 325°F/170°C or gas mark 3

First remove the meat from the birds and put the carcasses and bones into a pan. Add water, onion, carrot and bay leaf and simmer for 1½ hours. While this is cooking, cut the game meat and rump steak into even-sized pieces and put into the marinade. Leave in a cool place for about 6 hours.

Strain the stock, which will have reduced considerably, and you are ready to make up the pie. The longer you can leave the meat in the marinade the better since the wine will help to tenderise it. If it can be left overnight so much the better.

To make up the pie, melt the butter in a frying pan and fry the bacon for a few minutes. Then add the onions and fry till lightly browned. Now remove the meat from the marinade, drain and dry well. Fry in the pan with the onions and bacon till browned, then add the flour and stir in well. Season with salt and pepper and put into a $2\frac{1}{2}$ pt ($1\frac{1}{4}$ L) pie dish. Add marinade and fill up with stock. Cover with foil and put in a warm oven for 2 hours. Remove from the oven and leave to cool.

Roll out the pastry to fit the pie dish. Allow a double edge round the lip of the pie dish. Wet edges with water to make them stick. Decorate on top with pastry leaves and flute edges. Brush on top with egg and bake in a hot oven 425°F/220°C or gas mark 6 for 20–30 minutes till the pastry is browned and nicely risen.

STAR ROCK

Where the Angus glens open onto Strathmore there are several small agricultural towns like Blairgowrie and Kirriemuir. In Kirrie (as it is known locally) you can buy Star Rock, a traditional Angus sweet. The sticks are short and thin with a distinctive but undefinable flavour which is a well-kept secret.

This chewy rock was originally made by a stonemason who was blinded in 1833; the tradition is continued in a small shop in The Roods, Kirriemuir. As well as making the original rock here, home-made humbugs of various flavours are also on sale. Another variety of rock used to be made in Brechin, but this is no longer produced.

CARSE OF GOWRIE FRUIT

Nine-tenths of Scotland's raspberry crop is grown in the Strathmore area and along the coastal districts of Angus. The Carse of Gowrie, a narrow plain stretching from Perth to Dundee along the coast, is where the most intensive production of soft fruits, raspberries, strawberries and peas takes place. Low rainfall, freedom from spring frosts, prolonged summer sunshine and rich marine soil reclaimed from peat marsh all contribute to the prosperity of this industry.

Local towns, particularly Dundee, are centres of the jam-making, preserving and canning industries using locally grown produce. Much of the fresh crop is also transported to markets all over Britain. Raspberries, strawberries and blackcurrants of very fine quality are usually available (depending on the summer climate) towards the end of June and certainly in July and most of August.

Fresh Fruit Salad

2 lb fresh fruit including raspberries, strawberries and blackcurrants (1 kg)	Juice of 1 lemon
	2 tbsp brandy, rum or sherry
½ lb sugar (250 g)	½ oz blanched split almonds (15 g)
1 pt water (500 ml)	

Put the sugar and water into a pan and dissolve the sugar while bringing it to the boil. Boil for 10–15 minutes to make a syrup, leave to cool. Add the lemon juice and any other flavouring.

Prepare the fruit and add to the syrup with the almonds. Leave in a cool place for at least 2–3 hours, preferably overnight to allow the flavours to develop. Serve with fresh cream.

Raspberry and Strawberry Jam

In Scotland housewives generally make more jam than their English counterparts, Raspberry and Strawberry being the most popular varieties. Unlike the more traditional methods, which lose much of the original flavour of the fruit, this modern jam recipe (which came from a housewife in the Strathmore area) makes use of the deep-freeze in a method which really does preserve that fresh, sharp tang of the newly-ripe fruit.

3½ lb fresh raspberries (1.6 kg) or 3 lb strawberries (1.3 kg)	4 tbsp lemon juice (for raspberries only)
4 lb caster sugar (1.8 kg)	8 fl. oz liquid fruit pectin (225 g)

Put the rasps into a bowl, add sugar and lemon juice and stir to dissolve the sugar. Add the liquid pectin and stir for about two minutes. Ladle the mixture into small containers about 4 oz size (125 g) leaving ½" (1 cm) head space. Cover and leave at room temperature for about 24 hours or until set.

Place in the freezing compartment and use as a jam or filling for pies and tarts. Keep in the refrigerator once you have defrosted it and use within 2–3 weeks.

For the strawberries, the method is as above except that the sugar is left for 30 minutes on the strawberries and they are mashed very slightly. No lemon juice is used.

DUNDEE

Dundee Marmalade

The coincidence which links the town of Dundee with this very old preserve of European ancestry happened one day in the winter of 1700 when young James Keiller, a humble Dundee grocer, somewhat rashly bought up a cheap consignment of bitter Seville oranges that had arrived at the port.

His wife Janet had been making a preserve with quinces from an old family recipe of her mother's and when presented with this large quantity of oranges she simply substituted them for quinces and made up some pots of the attractive orange preserve. They were, like many grocers of the time, in the habit of making their own sweets so had plenty of large pans for boiling the preserve. She put them on the counter of their shop and people liked it so much they demanded more. In time the fame of the Dundee preserve spread further afield and Seville oranges were imported specially to make it.

Several generations later, in 1797, another Mrs Keiller and her son James finally felt confident enough to put the idea to the commercial test and built the world's first marmalade factory. Today more than half a million pounds of marmalade are eaten every day.

The word originated in the Portuguese and Spanish languages from their name for quinces – *marmelo*. The preserve made from them was called *marmelada* and the first mention of this word in Britain was in 1524 when Henry VIII noted with relish that a 'box of marmalade' had been presented to him.

Throughout the 16th and 17th centuries cookery books do mention this preserve being made with a variety of fruits, among them plums, dates, cherries, apricots and apples as well as quinces. The credit for first making a citrus-fruit marmalade must go to the noted epicure, scholar and traveller Sir Kenelm Digby (1603–1665). Having travelled widely in Italy and Spain, he introduced the idea of using oranges and lemons in a cookery book published posthumously in 1669.

Somehow this became popular in Scotland because in 1747 in his book *Tours of Scotland*, 1747, 1750, 1760, another epicurean traveller Bishop Richard Pococke (1704–1765) indicates the use of marmalade at breakfast. He noted that 'they always bring toasted bread, and besides, butter, honey and jelly of currants and preserved orange peel'.

By 1759 there was a recipe for it in the leading Scottish cookery book of the day *A New and Easy Method of Cookery,* by Mrs E. Cleland.

– To make a Marmalade of Oranges

Take your Oranges, grate them, cut them in Quarters, take the Skins off them, and take the Pulp from the Strings and Seeds; put the Skins in a pan of Spring-Water, Boil them till they are very tender, then take them out of the water, and cut them in very thin slices; beat some in a Marble Mortar, and leave the thin slices to boil by themselves. To every Pound of Oranges put a Pound of fine sugar; first wet the sugar in water, Boil it a good while, then put in Half of the pulp, keep the other half for the sliced Oranges; to every Mutchkin of the pulp you must put in a pound of Sugar likeways, then put in the grated Rind, boil till it is very clear, then put in Gallypots; when cold paper them.

It may have been this recipe, or one very similar, which was handed down from one Mrs Keiller to the next throughout the 18th century.

As a centre of the preserving industry in Scotland, Dundee was the natural place for marmalade-making to flourish. From the beginnings here have developed many modern varieties of many different flavours and textures. There are thick and thin ones, vintage varieties, some with whisky, as well as tangerine, lime and lemon ones.

Dundee Cake

Dundee is the only town in Scotland which has managed to produce two specialities (marmalade and cake) which are as well known south of the Border as they are north of it.

This recipe is a light fruit cake with very good keeping qualities and an excellent flavour. It rose to fame as a tea-time cake in the late 19th century and it has as its most distinctive feature whole almonds covering the top surface, which are gently roasted while the cake is baking.

8 oz butter (250 g)	4 oz raisins (125 g)
8 oz sugar (250 g)	2 oz mixed peel (50 g)
5 eggs	Zest of an orange or lemon
10 oz self-raising flour (300 g)	1 tbsp sherry or brandy or rum
Pinch of salt	Milk to mix
3 oz ground almonds (75 g)	2 oz blanched almonds for the top (50 g)
4 oz currants (125 g)	
4 oz sultanas (125 g)	

Preheat the oven to 350°F/180°C or gas mark 4

Put the butter and sugar into a bowl and warm slightly. At the same time break all the eggs into a bowl, beat together and warm them very slightly either in a very cool oven or in a warm place. Beat the butter and sugar together till they lighten in colour and become creamy. Beat in the warmed eggs gradually. Add some flour if necessary to prevent curdling.

Next, sift in the flour, salt and ground almonds. Stir in gently, then add the fruit, mixed peel, orange or lemon zest, sherry or brandy or rum and mix all this together with enough milk to make a fairly soft consistency.

Turn into a lined 7" (18 cm) round cake tin, level the top and cover with blanched almonds. Bake in a moderate oven for 2½ hours.

Montrose Cakes

4 oz self-raising flour (125 g)	1 dsp brandy 1 dsp rose-water	*These are typical Scottish tea-time delicacies with an unusual flavouring.*
4 oz caster sugar (125 g)	¼ nutmeg, grated	
4 oz butter (125 g)	2 eggs	
3 oz currants (75 g)		

Preheat the oven to 375°F/190°C or gas mark 5

Put the butter and sugar into a bowl and beat together till they lighten in colour and become creamy. Add eggs one at a time, beating well.

Now add the currants, brandy, rose-water and nutmeg and continue beating for another few minutes. Then stir in the flour. Half-fill greased patty tins or paper cases with the mixture. Bake for 10–15 minutes. Makes 22 cakes.

Angus Fruit Cake

1 lb plain flour (500 g)	2 heaped tsp bicarbonate of soda	*As well as soft fruits, apples, pears and plums ripen well in this area. This cake was obviously devised for using up the surplus apples. It is a moist cake with a sharp, spicy flavour which should not be kept more than a week.*
6 oz butter or margarine (175 g)	1 lb cooking apples, peeled, cored and sliced (500 g)	
1 egg		
½ pt buttermilk (¼ L)	5 oz golden syrup or honey (150 g)	
3 heaped tsp mixed spice		
1 heaped tsp cinnamon		

Preheat the oven to 350°F/180°C or gas mark 4

First put the syrup or honey into a pan and add the apples. Simmer the apples with the lid on until they are quite soft. Leave to cool.

Meanwhile sift the flour into a bowl and rub in the fat. Add the mixed spice, cinnamon and bicarbonate of soda. Make a well in the centre and add the egg, buttermilk and apples. Mix together to make a soft-dropping consistency. Turn into a lined 7" (18 cm) round cake tin and bake in a moderate oven for 1½ hours.

Possibly because the port of Dundee imported a great deal of almonds there are a number of recipes which use them, this time in a popular local sweet.

Angus Toffee

1½ lb granulated sugar (750 g)	1 oz butter (25 g)
2 oz ground almonds (50 g)	7 fl oz milk (200 ml)
	1 tsp almond essence

Melt butter in a pan. Add the ground almonds, sugar and milk. Stir till the sugar is dissolved. Bring to the boil and simmer till it reaches soft ball – 240°F/120°C. To test without a thermometer, drop some of the syrup into a cup of cold water and it should come together into a soft ball when ready. Remove from the heat and beat for about 5 minutes or until it becomes thick. Add the almond essence and pour into a shallow baking tin. Cut up when almost cold.

Arbroath Smokies

Along the Angus and Kincardine coast are many small fishing ports, now mostly obsolete with one or two exceptions. Among them, a few miles north of Arbroath, the picturesque village of Auchmithie sits perched on the edge of a steep sea cliff with a harbour, no longer in use, down below. This is where the Arbroath Smokie originated. Fish wives using upturned barrels produced the *Auchmithie Luckens, Closefish,* or *Pinwiddies,* as they were variously called. Today they are known simply as *Smokies* and none of these old names has survived.

For the cure, fresh haddocks of the same size are gutted, headed and left whole. They are then dry-salted for about one hour, tied in pairs by the tails and hung over hot smoke for 40–50 minutes. The result is a copper-coloured, mildly smoked cooked fish.

Since the fish is already cooked it can be eaten cold with brown bread and butter and lemon, or spread with butter, wrapped in foil and heated up in the oven. It is often served with a baked or boiled jacket potato as a favourite high-tea dish.

With a strong fishing tradition, soups and broths using the leftover bones and heads are typical examples of Scottish thriftiness.

Although it has a humble beginning, this particular soup is finished with the French egg

Angus Fish Soup

6 fresh haddock heads	Salt and pepper
2 pts water (1 L)	2 oz butter (50 g)
1 small carrot	2 oz flour (50 g)
1 slice turnip	½ pt milk (250 ml)
1 stick celery	1 egg yolk
3–4 sprigs of parsley	3 tbsp double cream

Garnish – 1 tbsp chopped parsley

Rinse the heads and place in a pan with the cold water, bring to the boil and skim. Add vegetables, parsley and seasoning. Simmer till the vegetables are tender. Strain. Melt the butter in a pan and add flour to make a white roux. Gradually add the strained broth and then the milk. Cook for a few minutes. Season, blend in the egg yolk and cream and heat through but do not boil. Serve immediately, garnished with some parsley.

FIFE

The Fife peninsula has a peaceful past compared with the rest of Scotland. It was partly the long barrier of the Ochil hills which protected it from the wasteful invasions and wars which so devastated the rest of the country. This fortunate peninsula was allowed to prosper, particularly along the rich coastal 'golden fringe' which attracted seven early monasteries, among them St Andrews, the oldest University town in Scotland, and Dunfermline, once the capital.

The richest farming area is along the coast and in Stratheden where the dry, sunnier east coast climate combines with good soil. Oats and barley were originally the main crops grown – wheat, potatoes and turnips came later.

Again along the coast there are many old fishing villages and little ports which at one time traded with Europe, the Baltic and the Mediterranean. Fishing was at its height in the 19th century, with Burntisland alone supporting five hundred boats. The picturesque villages with their red-tiled fisher houses and outside stairs to the lofts above, where the nets were kept, are a sad reminder of decline in a local industry. The significant ports now are Anstruther, Crail, Pittenweem and St Monance, once centres of the herring industry but now increasingly interested in white fish, lobsters and crabs.

and cream thickening which makes it a delicate light soup in contrast to the heavier broths.

It seems quite possible that this soup, like Friar's Chicken in the Borders, with a similar egg and cream thickening, was introduced to this area by the medieval French monks who settled in large numbers here as well as in the Borders.

'A reuch Scots blanket wi' a fringe o' gowd' (James V)

Partan Bree

1 large cooked crab	¼ pt single cream
(about 2–3 lb, 1–1½ kg)	(125 ml)
2 oz rice (50 g)	Anchovy essence to taste
1 pt milk (600 ml)	Salt and pepper
1 pt water (600 ml)	

Garnish – Chopped parsley

Remove all the meat from the crab, keeping the claw meat separate. Put the rice in a pan with the milk and water. Cook till the rice is tender.

This is more of a national than a regional dish, but it is made in this area whenever crabs are plentiful. Crabs are known throughout Scotland by their Gaelic name (partan) and bree simply means 'liquid' or gravy.

The season lasts from January to October and the crabs are usually boiled by the

31

fishmonger. To cook them if they are live, plunge them into a large pan of boiling water and simmer for 20 minutes. They can weigh anything from 1½–8 lb, but for quality the best weight is about 3 lb (1.4 kg). It is illegal to offer for sale crabs less than 4½" (10 cm) in breadth across the broad part of the back, or any crab carrying spawn (known as 'berried' crabs).

There is a long history of fine-quality seed potatoes as well as 'earlies' in this area along the coast. Further inland, on the rough moorland, sheep produce excellent mutton which combines with the potatoes in this substantial peasant-style broth.

Put the rice and some of the cooking liquid into a liquidiser with all the crab meat except the meat from the claws. Make into a fine purée or put all this through a sieve. Return purée to the soup and add anchovy essence and cream.

Season and adjust the consistency with more milk if necessary. Add claw meat and some finely chopped parsley. Heat through but do not boil. Serve in heated soup bowls.

Largo Potato Soup

1 lb neck of mutton (½ kg)	1¼ lb finely chopped onions (625 g)
4 pt water (2 L)	1½ lb sliced potatoes (750 g)
4 oz finely chopped carrots (125 g)	Salt and pepper

Garnish – Chopped parsley

Put the mutton in a pan with water. Bring to the boil and skim. Add carrots and onions, season with salt and pepper and simmer for 2 hours.

Add the potatoes 30 minutes before the end. Lift out meat, remove bones and any excess fat. Chop up finely and return to the soup. Check seasoning and serve garnished with parsley.

The following three recipes are among the handful of regional Scottish dishes which use pig. In the rich Lowland farming areas such as this one it was more common to keep pigs than in Highlands, but in only a few areas have pork specialities developed.

In the pie and the Kilmeny Kail the bacon is used with rabbit, which was plentiful though not always popular. The bacon in these dishes gives the rabbit some much-needed flavour.

Kingdom of Fife Pie

1 young rabbit approx 1¼ lb (625 g)	2 oz fine white bread-crumbs (50 g)
1 lb bacon in a piece (500 g)	2 oz fat bacon, finely chopped (50 g)
¼ of a grated nutmeg	1 oz parsley, finely chopped (25 g)
Salt and pepper	A few sprigs of lemon thyme
4 tbsp dry white wine	¼ of a grated nutmeg
¼ pt stock or water (125 ml)	1 egg
8 oz puff pastry (250 g)	
Egg for brushing	

For the stuffing – Rabbit liver, finely chopped

Preheat the oven to 375°F/190°C or gas mark 5

Joint the rabbit, cover with cold water and leave for 1 hour. Cut up the bacon into 1" (2½ cm) pieces. Mix the stuffing ingredients together and bind with egg. Shape into balls. Pack the rabbit and bacon into a 2½ pt (1¼ L) pie dish, seasoning with nutmeg, salt and pepper. Fill up the spaces with the stuffing balls and then add the stock or water and wine. Cover with puff pastry, brush with egg and make some ventilation holes. Bake for 1 hour.

Fife Broth

1 lb pork ribs (500 g)　　$\frac{1}{2}$ lb potatoes (250 g)
$2\frac{1}{2}$ pt water ($1\frac{1}{4}$ L)　　Salt and pepper
$1\frac{1}{2}$ oz barley (40 g)

Garnish – Parsley

Put the ribs into a pan with water and bring to the boil. Skim and add barley and potatoes. Simmer for 2–$2\frac{1}{2}$ hours. Remove the ribs and cut off the meat. Dice finely and return to the soup. Check seasoning, garnish with parsley and serve.

Kilmeny Kail

1 young rabbit approx　　Salt and pepper
　$1\frac{1}{4}$ lb (625 g)　　1 lb greens, cabbage and/
1 lb bacon in a piece　　　or kail, finely chopped
　(500 g)　　　　　　　(500 g)
2 pts water (1 L)

Clean the rabbit well and cut into pieces. Put into a large pot with the bacon. Cover with water, bring to the boil, skim and simmer for 2–3 hours. When the meat is cooked, add the greens and simmer for another 10–15 minutes. Remove the rabbit and pork and serve separately. Dice a little of the meat and return it to the soup for garnish. Check seasoning, adjust consistency and serve with oatcakes.

Fife Bannocks

6 oz plain flour (175 g)　　1 tsp cream of tartar
$\frac{1}{2}$ oz butter (15 g)　　　1 dsp sugar
4 oz fine oatmeal (125 g)　Pinch of salt
1 tsp bicarbonate of soda　Buttermilk to mix

This is a local recipe for the type of bannock which used to be staple fare all over Scotland. Since wheat was grown in this area it is not surprising to find a higher proportion than in its Highland counterpart.

Preheat the girdle – it should feel fairly hot if you hold your hand over it about an inch from the surface.

Sift the flour and rub in the butter, add oatmeal, soda, and cream of tartar, sugar and salt and mix with buttermilk to a fairly stiff dough.

　Turn out onto a floured board, dust with flour and roll out into a round $\frac{1}{2}''$ thick (1 cm). Divide into 8 and cook on both sides on a hot girdle till nicely browned. Serve warm with crowdie and raspberry or strawberry jam.

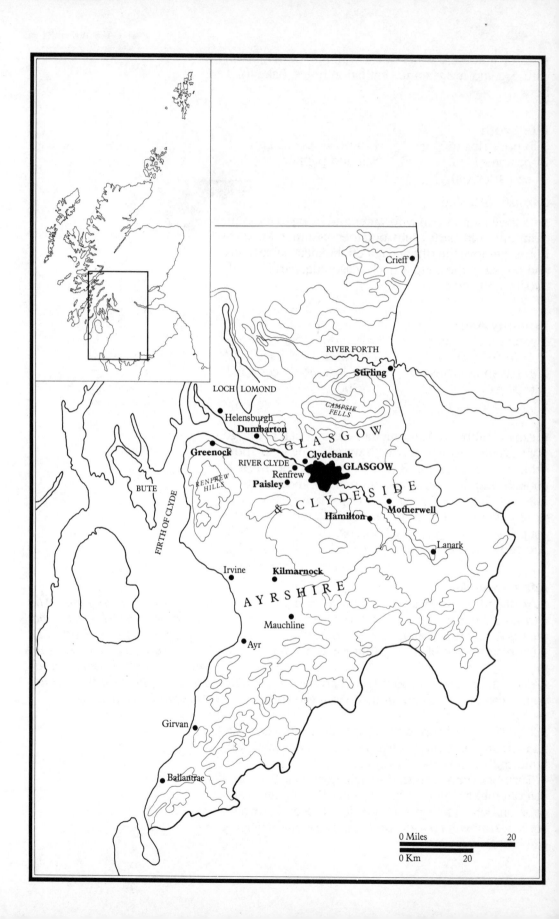

Crieff

RIVER FORTH

Stirling

LOCH LOMOND

CAMPSIE FELLS

Helensburgh

Dumbarton

G L A S G O W

Greenock

Clydebank

RIVER CLYDE

GLASGOW

Renfrew

BUTE

RENFREW HILLS

Paisley

& C L Y D E S I D E

Motherwell

FIRTH OF CLYDE

Hamilton

Lanark

Irvine

Kilmarnock

A Y R S H I R E

Mauchline

Ayr

Girvan

Ballantrae

0 Miles 20

0 Km 20

3. Glasgow and Clydeside

Before its power and wealth began to flourish in the 18th century, Glasgow was a small fishing village; the Clyde was virtually non-navigable, except by barge, and pack-horses linked Glasgow with Irvine – its main sea port. Today a third of Scotland's people live and work in this area, still one of Britain's major manufacturing provinces, and it is several centuries since the produce of the land had any direct effect on what its people were eating.

THE HIGHLAND IMMIGRATION

It was after free access to the American colonies in 1707 that trade and industry grew and flourished here. A vast rural population left the land, abandoned their old habits and traditions, and developed quite new ones in an entirely different environment. Most of this new urban population was Celtic Highlanders or Celtic Irish. They brought with them a simple but sound tradition of boiling and stewing, with oatmeal and milk dishes predominating. How much of this survived depended on their standard of living. If housing was bad and cooking facilities limited; if factory working wives and girls had only a limited time to prepare food and mothers were not able to pass on their traditions to their daughters; if incomes were so low that only the barest essentials were possible, then traditional dishes were bound to disappear – and many of them did.

THE GROWTH OF RETAILING

The era of the oatmeal and milk tradition was fading and a new tea-and-white-bread one was taking its place. Dependence on food retailers was growing and some huge Victorian Glasgow grocery businesses developed as a direct result.

Perhaps the most famous of all the multiple retailers, as they were known, was Thomas Lipton, who opened his first provision shop in Stobcross Street in 1871. He attracted customers with his cut-price foods, initially butter, cheese, bacon, eggs and ham which he bought cheaply from Ireland, thus undercutting his rivals. These methods, plus Lipton's flair for advertising, made him into the most successful food retailer of the period. It was the tea trade which made his name famous in the next quarter of a century: he bought his own plantations in Ceylon and sold his own brands of tea. By 1898 he had 400 shops throughout the world, as well as many factories producing a wide range of Lipton groceries.

Among the many food imports which came up the River Clyde in the 19th century, tea from the East and sugar from the West Indies probably had the greatest influence on the pattern of urban eating. In 1865 the duty on tea was reduced from 1/10d per lb to 6d per lb, which made it no longer a rich man's luxury but available to the mass of the population. There was no tea-drinking tradition common to all; instead many varieties developed to suit different occasions and needs.

HIGH TEA

When industrial workers ate dinner in the middle of the day the meal at night came to be called High Tea. This was a substantial meal with a main course of perhaps cold-cooked meats, smoked fish, potted meats or pies from the grocer, cakes, scones or pancakes from the baker accompanied by plenty of strong tea, bread, butter and jam.

Saturday-night teas were the most popular of the week: families came together and a special spread was laid with lots of scones. Pancakes, sweet, sticky cakes and often cooked foods like pies, fish and chips or boiled ham were firm favourites. This Saturday night tea-ritual was the Scots equivalent of the English Sunday Lunch. Sundays in Scotland were for going to church.

Fresh fruit was always plentiful in Glasgow and was sold from barrows in the streets in large quantities. On Saturdays Parliamentary Road was adorned with fruit barrows from end to end. Some of the fruit came from the fruit and market-gardening area of the Clyde valley between Lanark and Motherwell but much of it was imported.

THE BIRTH OF THE TEA ROOM

The nostalgic memory of Miss Cranston and her tea rooms is still strong. Those Glaswegians who enjoyed the experience now regret that such a tradition should have died. The original and beautiful decorations have passed into architectural histories and now are museum items in the Glasgow Art Galleries.

Miss Cranston was a pioneer of the tea room, which had not existed before the 1880s. Men drank in coffee houses, clubs and taverns; women stayed at home and had tea parties with their friends – until Catherine Cranston, daughter of a hotel proprietor, rented a half-shop in Argyle Street and opened the Crown Lunch and

Tea Rooms. From this small beginning in 1884 the business grew and developed as the fashionable and rising middle classes seized the opportunity to parade in public rather than at home. Women were the main customers, though not exclusively so, since Miss Cranston's schemes went much further than just simple tea rooms. She provided special rooms for smoking, playing chess, dominoes and billiards, also a reading room which allowed people to relax in a congenial atmosphere.

About the turn of the century, she bought a series of lofty apartments in Ingram Street for conversion to a suite of fashionable tea rooms and dining rooms. Charles Rennie Mackintosh created the interiors of her premises over the next twenty years, establishing a new style which led to much of his personal fame. Together with his wife, Margaret MacDonald, and another contemporary, George Walton, their work ranged from transforming whole interiors to designing detailed trimmings like cutlery, wall lamps, coat-stands and domino tables.

Taking its name from the Sauchie Haugh, 'the low ground where the saughs or willows grow', Sauchiehall Street was the scene of the most famous Cranston establishment – The Willow Tea Rooms, including the famous Room de Luxe on the first floor with its elegant furniture and mirrored walls. The specialities of these tea rooms were high teas and afternoon teas, and the Scottish baking tradition flourished in this setting. A special three-tier cake stand was the centrepiece of every table and on it were to be found freshly made light tea-breads, particularly scones and pancakes as well as all kinds of dainty cakes. To accompany this, the main meal dish was a simple affair. Cold cooked or potted meats, poached white fish with a poached egg, fried haddock and chips, a smokie or perhaps a kipper.

The very high standards of food and service which Miss Cranston achieved, together with an original setting, brought a special brightness to this industrial city of the West, making the tea room habit not only famous but openly imitated throughout the rest of Britain.

COOKED FOODS

The trade in cooked foods was a growing one at this period in all the developing industrial areas. These foods were a vital part of the city diet, whether they were sold in the streets, in shops, at markets, in parks or at fairs or races, since they often supplied a whole day's meals for labouring boys and girls with a working mother.

Actual selling and eating of cooked foods in the streets, as was the custom in the urban areas of England, particularly London, was not so common north of the Border. Presumably the colder climate had something to do with this, since it seems that the street food specialities were mainly consumed in shops or under canvas cover at markets.

Italian immigrants in Glasgow were the people who provided much of the cooked or prepared foods. They brought with them the ice-cream-making expertise which made them famous, but they also specialised in Hot Peas and Vinegar with Chips, Hot Pies and Boiled Mussels and Whelks. The Fish and Chip combination is thought to have originated in the English Midlands, although it travelled to Scotland very quickly and soon became one of the staple cooked foods of the period.

A keen supporter of Clyde football club is said to have been responsible for the Glasgow custom of putting raspberry-flavoured syrup on top of an ice-cream cone. In his enthusiasm he is supposed to have persuaded a local 'Taly' (Italian café) to make cones look like the red and white colours of 'the team' and this came to be known after him as a MacCallum. Whatever the origins of the custom, a squirt of raspberry syrup is still offered when you buy a cone in Glasgow.

Scotch Pies

For the filling –
½ lb minced lean mutton (250 g)
1 medium onion, finely chopped
½ oz lard (12 g)
½ pt water (300 ml)
1 tbsp chopped parsley

½ level tsp salt
¼ level tsp pepper
1 dsp flour
For the pastry –
2 oz beef dripping (50 g)
¼ pt water (150 ml)
8 oz plain flour (250 g)
½ level tsp salt

Preheat the oven to 350°F/180°C or gas mark 4

To make the filling, melt the lard in a pan and add the onion, then fry gently till cooked – but not brown. Now add the mince and break up with a fork till it is all separated. Add water and cook for 15–20 minutes. Now stir in the flour to thicken. Add the seasoning and parsley and leave to cool.

Make up the pastry by melting the dripping in a pan

These small mutton pies, with their crust standing up round them about ½" above the filling, were always a very popular fast food for working people in Glasgow. They are still to be found in all bakers shops there, though they are not so easy to find now in some other parts of Scotland. The rim above the meat was often filled with hot gravy, peas or beans and a spoonful of potato to make a complete meal. They are always served piping hot. Bakers keep them in a hot cupboard – they are not good cold.

There used to be an

establishment in the Candleriggs run by an old Glasgow character, Grannie Black, which was renowned far and wide for its 'Twopenny Mutton Pies'.

with water. Bring to the boil. Meanwhile sift the flour and salt into a bowl and make a well in the centre. Pour in the liquid and mix together with a knife until it is cool enough to handle.

Knead into a soft, pliable dough and remove one-third of it for the lids, then put in a warm place to keep soft. Divide the rest into 6 pieces, depending on the size of the pies. They are usually about 3–3½" (7.5–8.5 cm) in diameter by 1¼–1½" deep (3–4 cm) with a ½" (1 cm) rim of pastry standing up above the lid. Roll out the six rounds and fit into pie rings or tins. The pastry should be fairly thin. Fill with meat and then roll out the lids. Cut a small circle out of each lid for the steam to escape through and place on top of meat mixture. Bake for 40–45 minutes.

Unlike their English counterparts, who rather despised soup as food for the poorhouse, the urban population in Scotland has preserved the broth tradition, probably because this sort of dish was always easy to prepare, did not need much attention while cooking and also provided food for several days.

This is a variety of the substantial Scotch Broth, using broad or butter beans which are popular here. The meat is eaten hot one day with some of the 'bree' (cooking liquor) and the soup drunk the next when the flavour has matured.

Glasgow Broth

Marrow bone	1 lb turnip, diced finely
2 qts water (2 L)	(500 g)
1½–2 lb piece of boiling	1 leek
beef (750 g–1 kg)	1 lb carrots, diced
4 oz barley (125 g)	finely (500 g)
½ lb dried peas steeped	Few sticks of celery
for several hours	Salt and pepper
or overnight (250 g)	
½ lb butter beans steeped	
for several hours	
or overnight (250 g)	

Garnish –
Parsley, chopped

Put cold water into a very large pan and add the bone, beef seasoning and barley. Bring to the boil, skim, cover and simmer for 2 hours.

Take out beef and the bone, then add beans and peas. Add carrot and turnip and bring to the boil. Simmer for about 2 hours till the beans and peas are soft. Add the celery and leek for the last half hour. Add parsley just before serving. It can be put into the heated soup plate and the soup poured on top. Serves 8–12.

Tripe in Glasgow was prepared by steaming for about 8 hours in a stone jar or steamer with a knuckle or marrow bone. When it cooled, the tripe was set

Glasgow Tripe

1½ lb tripe (750 g)	1 oz flour (25 g)
3–4 medium onions,	Salt and pepper
chopped	2 tbsp double cream
1 oz butter (25 g)	

Garnish – Parsley

Preheat the oven to 325°F/170°C or gas mark 3

Cut up the tripe roughly into 1″ (2.5 cm) squares. Put into a 2½ pt (1¼ L) pie dish or casserole and add onions, salt and pepper. Dot with some butter on top. Cover tightly and place in a moderate oven for 1½–2 hours. Half an hour before it is ready, remove from the oven and blend some of the hot liquid with the flour. Return to the oven and finish the cooking. To finish, stir in some cream and check seasoning. Garnish with parsley and serve with baked jacket potatoes.

in its own jelly and pieces of this were used as required. Usually a very thick onion sauce was made and then jellied tripe added. Tripe stock was traditionally used for making potato soup.

Today the butcher does the initial eight-hour boiling, so the tripe we use needs only about another two hours' cooking. This method uses no liquid to cook the tripe, but with a little butter and some onions it will cook very well in its own juices.

GLASGOW SWEETIES
The Scots are noted for their sweet tooth and their skill in sweetie-making. Sweetie wives used to make their own sweets and sell them in the streets and markets. Since sugar was one of Glasgow's major imports and sugar-refining an important industry in the area there were plenty of sweets available and many local varieties developed.

In the latter half of the nineteenth century a local character, known as Ball Allan – The Candy King of Glasgow, made a variety known as *Cheugh Jeans*. *Cheugh* means 'chewey' and they were of many different flavours: clove, cinnamon, peppermint, ginger. This chocolate variety was very popular, and it is certainly cheugh.

Glasgow Toffee

4 oz butter (125 g)	6 oz golden syrup (175 g)
4 oz white sugar (125 g)	1½ oz plain chocolate
4 oz brown sugar (125 g)	(75 g)
¼ pt milk (150 ml)	½ tsp vanilla essence

Melt butter in a large pan and then add sugar, milk, syrup and chocolate, broken in pieces. Heat up gradually to dissolve the sugar and then bring to the boil. Boil rapidly, stirring all the time till it reaches 250°F/130°C or until some of the toffee forms a hard ball when tested in a cup of cold water.

Remove from the heat and let it settle. Add the vanilla and pour into a shallow tin. Leave till it is almost set before cutting. Wrap in wax paper.

This is a more sophisticated and delicate confection, as befits the pretentions of this leisured and wealthy haven sited at a convenient distance from the industrial centres. More like a fudge than a toffee, it has a rich, creamy flavour and is now one of the most popular home-made sweeties.

Helensburgh Toffee

4 oz butter (125 g)	1 tbsp syrup
$\frac{1}{4}$ pt water or milk (125 g)	7$\frac{1}{2}$ fl oz tin condensed milk (200 ml)
2 lb granulated sugar (1 kg)	Vanilla essence
	Walnut halves

Put the butter and water into a large pan and heat till the butter is melted. Add sugar and syrup and heat gently till the sugar is dissolved. Do not boil at this stage. Now add the condensed milk and bring gradually to simmering point. Stir all the time till the temperature reaches 240°F/120°C or until some of the syrup forms a soft ball when tested in a cup of cold water.

Remove from the heat, allow to settle and add vanilla essence. Now the mixture has to be beaten quite vigorously till it changes texture and colour. When it is ready to pour out, it should be slightly lighter in colour. The texture should have changed from smooth to slightly grained. As it begins to grain it gets thicker, so do not wait too long before pouring into a greased baking tin.

TO DRINK

This recipe comes from a nineteenth-century handwritten cookery notebook found among some books at the Glasgow 'Barrows' (open-air weekend market). Rum punch was very popular among the city businessmen at this time. Rum was a Glasgow import, brandy an Edinburgh one: the original recipe used 4 pints.

Glasgow Punch

$\frac{1}{2}$ pt rum or brandy ($\frac{1}{4}$ L)	1$\frac{1}{2}$ pints water ($\frac{3}{4}$ L)
1 orange	6 oz caster sugar (200 g)
1 lemon	

Remove the zest from the orange and lemon and add to the rum or brandy. Cover and steep for 24 hours.

Put water into a pan and add sugar, bring to the boil and reduce to half by boiling rapidly without a lid on the pan. Leave the syrup to cool then add the orange and lemon juice. Strain the rum or brandy onto this and bottle. It was usually taken hot with water before drinking.

Quick Punch

Put 1 tbsp of icing sugar into a large tumbler. Add the juice of 1 lemon and about 2$\frac{1}{2}$ fl oz (60 ml) of rum. Fill with ice and stir.

Het Pint

1 pint mild ale or red
  wine ($\frac{1}{2}$ L)
$\frac{1}{4}$ whole nutmeg
Sugar to taste

1 egg, beaten
2$\frac{1}{2}$ fl oz whisky or brandy
  ($\frac{3}{4}$ L)

Put the ale or red wine into a pan, grate in the nutmeg and add sugar to taste. Heat to almost boiling point. Remove from the heat and pour over the egg, stirring all the time. Strain and add whisky or brandy. Heat through again but do not boil, or the egg will curdle. Pour from the pan to a heated jug or kettle briskly several times till it has a good head of froth. Drink hot.

This was the aromatic drink which perfumed the streets of Glasgow and Edinburgh at New Year a hundred years ago. It was made up very hot before the 'First Fits' left home and then poured into a gleaming copper kettle. A cup-bearer accompanied the kettle-carrier, and all and sundry were offered a drink. Accounts of what actually went into it vary though it is quite clear that Edinburgh people made one with a variety of ingredients including wine and brandy, while the less sophisticated Glasgow one contained mild ale and whisky. Whatever the combination, it must have been a cup that cheered many a frozen reveller as the night wore on.

'But in its most superior form the 'het pint'' was compounded of port, sherry, or madeira, mulled with cardamons, cloves, nutmeg, ginger, cinnamon and coriander, flavoured with sugar and frothy with whipped eggs, poured hot and steaming into the copper kettles in which it was carried . . .' (Old Edinburgh Taverns by Marie W. Smart).

BAKING

Apple Frushie

8 oz cooking apples (250 g)
3 tsp rose water
2 oz clear honey (50 g)
For the pastry –
8 oz flour (200 g)

2 oz margarine (50 g)
2 oz lard (50 g)
Salt
Water to mix

Preheat the oven to 400°F/200°C or gas mark 4

To make the pastry, sift the flour into a bowl and add salt. Rub in margarine and lard till the mixture is like fine breadcrumbs. Sprinkle in a little water and mix to a stiff dough with a round-bladed knife. Leave aside in a cool place to rest for five minutes.

Roll out pastry on a floured board and line a greased 9$\frac{1}{2}$" (24 cm) enamel plate. Cut off scraps and roll out to make strips for the top of the pie. Peel, core and slice the apples very thinly. Spread them out on the base of the plate. Sprinkle with rose water and pour honey evenly over the apples. Lay strips on top of apples to make a lattice design. Seal with a little water at the edges. Bake in a hot oven for 25–30 minutes. When cooked, sprinkle with caster sugar and serve hot with cream.

This is a variety of open fruit tart, usually made with apples or greengages, which is popular in the West of Scotland. Frushie is an old Scots word meaning 'brittle' or 'crumbly', which applies to the pastry. It is a good example of the Victorian love of ornamentation.

4. *Ayrshire*

AYRSHIRE FARMING

The lowlands of Ayrshire form a crescent shape along about seventy miles of the Firth of Clyde coast. The warm, wet winds which blow in from the sea plus the clay and heavy loam soil most suitable for growing grass have combined to grow the most succulent pasture and to make this the largest dairying district in Scotland. Over 63,000 dairy cattle in Ayrshire produce over 50 million gallons of milk annually.

For three centuries now this area has been noted for its dairy cows, and the breed of cattle which has evolved today is prized throughout the world for the quality and quantity of its milk supplies. The cows are a light to deep cherry-red, mahogany-brown, or a combination of these colours mottled with white, or white alone. Distinctive red-and-white markings are preferred by breeders to black or brindle. The horns are small, set wide apart at the base and have a graceful curve inwards. Most of the vast quantity of milk produced goes to the nearby urban areas, but there is enough left over to supply a thriving creamery industry making butter, cheese and other milk products.

CHEESE-MAKING

Throughout the South-West and on some islands, the major Scottish creameries produce a cheddar-type cheese as well as some of the less mature, softer and mellower *Ayrshire Dunlop*. There are creameries at Mauchline and further south in Campbeltown, and also on the islands of Bute, Arran, Islay and Gigha.

The *Ayrshire Dunlop* is thought to have originated in the 17th century when cheese-making was very much a home-made, rule-of-thumb affair for the farmers' wives and daughters. Some were obviously more expert and observant than others. Young Barbara Gilmore, an Ayrshire farmer's daughter, found herself in Ireland, fleeing persecution as a Covenanter. She studied and learned the more advanced methods of cheese-making from the Irish. When she returned to her home area of Dunlop she started making cheese with sweet milk rather than sour, and this soon became the custom throughout the area. This original Dunlop was common until the 19th century when the Highland Agricultural Society thought the quality was inferior and encouraged improvement in Scottish cheese-making.

In 1854 the Ayrshire Agricultural Association sent two of their members to England to discover the best way of making cheese. The next year a Somerset farmer and his wife were employed to make Cheddar-type cheese in Ayrshire and the new method was widely adopted throughout the South-West. From then on Glasgow merchants stopped buying fine English Cheddar for their wealthy and discerning customers and started selling the *Ayrshire Dunlop* which was, by now, a Cheddar-type cheese – but still with its own distinctive flavour.

AYRSHIRE BACON

Pigs are traditionally kept in any dairying areas since they use up the milk leftovers. In Scotland there has been much less of a pig tradition than in England, where every region has its pig specialities. But in Ayrshire a traditional bacon cure with a considerable reputation has developed. This method uses the whole side of the pig, so that the back or cutlet part and the streaky part are not separated. The side is boned, then traditionally brined in a pickle including soft brown sugar. It is then skinned and rolled up tightly with the fat side outwards and tied. It is not smoked, so the fat is soft and cream-coloured. Pieces of the roll are sometimes boiled and served cold, but it is usually cut in very thin rashers and grilled.

This popular dish (made from bacon scraps) was traditionally boiled in a cloth, the advantage of this method being that it does not dry out. At the same time, some of the flavour seeps into the water, so use foil or greaseproof paper within a cloth. Alternatively the roll can be put in a greased earthenware dish, covered tightly, set in a few inches of water and baked in the oven (350°F/180°C for 1 hour).

Ayrshire Meat Roll

1 lb Ayrshire bacon, minced (500 g)	¼ nutmeg, grated
1 lb stewing steak, minced (500 g)	2 eggs
6 oz fine white bread-crumbs (150 g)	1 medium onion, finely chopped
	Salt and freshly ground black pepper

Mix all the ingredients together thoroughly and then roll into a sausage-shape on a floured board. Wrap up in foil or greaseproof paper and tie securely in a scalded cotton or linen cloth. Boil for 2 hours – for full details see recipe for Aberdeen Sausage (p. 74). When cooked, roll in browned crumbs and serve hot or cold.

FISHING

South of the town of Ayr is the district of Carrick where, in contrast to the sandy bays to the north, old hard rocks reach down to the sea making a rugged, rocky coastline most suited to sheltered fishing harbours. The closely-knit fishing communities of Ayr, Dunure, Maidens, Girvan and Ballantrae have traditionally fished for salmon, particularly at the mouths of the rivers Ayr, Doon, Girvan and Stinchar; for lobsters and crabs all along the coast, and for herring and white fish in the waters of the Firth of Forth, Loch Fyne and further north and west.

Despite the decline generally in the industry, it is still important, with Ayr now the largest centre. Traditionally most of the catch was sent inland to the large urban markets; in Glasgow Loch Fyne herring were prized for their size and quality. Because of their plumpness they were jokingly referred to as Glasgow Magistrates or Baillies. They were usually stuffed with a herb and breadcrumb mixture and then pickled in vinegar.

Across the Firth from Ayrshire, people on the island of Arran also fished for a living and, as in all fishing communities, the families found themselves eating a great deal of their catch. Most of it was simply cooked, but one Arran housewife's recipe has emerged which obviously evolved out of the need to do something more interesting with cod. The combination of Cod and

Cod with mustard sauce

1½ lb cod fillets (¾ kg)	¼ pt milk (125 ml)
¾ pt water (375 ml)	1 tsp powdered English mustard
1 medium onion, finely chopped	2 tbsp lemon juice
1 oz flour (25 g)	3 tbsp chopped parsley
1 oz butter (25 g)	Salt and pepper

Cut the cod into eight even-sized pieces and put into a pan. Add parsley and onion and pour in water. Season with salt and pepper and bring gently to simmering point. Simmer for about 5 minutes.

Melt butter in another pan and add flour. Cook for a few minutes without colouring and, when the cod is cooked, pour all the cooking liquor gradually into the roux, stirring all the time. Add the milk and bring to the boil. Simmer for about five minutes then add the final flavouring. Put the mustard into a small bowl and blend to a paste with some of the sauce. Add the lemon juice and pour this mixture into the sauce. Check seasoning and pour over the fish. Serve immediately with stovies or baked potatoes and butter. If you keep this dish hot for any length of time before serving, the mustard will lose its flavour.

Mustard is an old Norse one which is found in other areas of Scotland with Norse ancestry. Here the addition of lemon juice gives the dish an added sharpness which combines well with the other flavours.

It is served with Arran potatoes which are well known for their fine quality. Many varieties have originated here which are now grown in many other parts of the country. The eating quality of cod is best from June through the winter till the beginning of March.

Ayrshire Shortbread

8 oz flour (225 g)	4 oz caster sugar (100 g)
1 tbsp rice flour	Yolk of egg
4 oz butter (100 g)	2 tbsp cream

Preheat the oven to 350°F/180°C or gas mark 4

It is perhaps significant, in a milk-producing area, that this shortbread should use cream. It seems to be the only area where this is common.

Sieve the flour and rice flour together into a bowl. Rub in butter and add sugar. Make a well in the centre and add the egg yolk and cream. Knead together lightly to make a fairly stiff dough. Divide into three pieces and roll into sausage-shapes about 1½" (4 cm) in diameter. Put into a cool place and leave for several hours or overnight. Cut into rounds ¼" thick (½ cm), place on a greased baking sheet and bake for 10–15 minutes.

Sweet Haggis

¾ lb medium oatmeal (350 g)	4 oz currants (125 g)
4 oz plain flour (125 g)	4 oz raisins (125 g)
¾ lb suet, finely chopped (350 g)	Salt and pepper
4 oz soft brown sugar (125 g)	Water to mix

Put all the dry ingredients into a bowl and mix with water. Put into a greased pudding bowl, cover and steam for 3–4 hours. Serve hot in slices. The remainder can later be cut in thick slices and fried with bacon or wrapped in foil and reheated in the oven.

This particular recipe originated in Kilmarnock and was a favourite Saturday night High Tea dish when newly boiled. It was usually put on at dinner time, in the middle of the day, before everyone in the family went out for the afternoon. When they came home the hot steaming pudding was a comforting sight which warmed and fed them on a cold winter's night. Leftovers also supplied substantial breakfasts, fried with thin rashers of Ayrshire bacon.

5. The Border Counties

As the main entry point from England, this area has seen more of its share of action throughout Scotland's troubled history. The Cheviot Hills were not an effective barrier in times of war but rather a convenient lookout for English invaders, who saw from their sheltered positions some of the richest and most productive lands of Scotland.

THE BORDER ABBEYS

In many places today there is still evidence of the effects of these wars with England, particularly in the sad but beautiful ruins of the Border abbeys.

Cistercian and Benedictine monks, who came to Scotland in the 11th and 12th centuries, built these abbeys and established a farming tradition with new methods completely unknown to the Scots. The sheep-farming tradition they developed was perhaps the most important, and the textile industry of the riverside towns owes its origins to the early stocking of the hills with sheep. The Border area, blessed with the finest alluvial soils, was also suitable for wheat, oats and barley. The monks kept cows, pigs and sheep in their self-supporting communities as well as enjoying the plentiful river salmon.

History has shaped this region in a way which gives it a colour and distinction, strongly expressed in the character of Border people. Sir Walter Scott, who worked to stimulate a general revival in Scottish self-awareness, was especially dedicated to preserving the stirring but often sad stories of Border history, and made his home at Abbotsford near Melrose.

MEG DODS

As a gesture towards preserving Scottish customs Scott was instrumental in making famous the fictional character Mistress Margaret Dods, whose cookery book was celebrated as the authority on traditional Scottish cookery in the nineteenth century. This book, *The Cook and Housewife's Manual,* or 'Meg Dods' Cookery' as it was popularly known, was actually compiled and written by Mrs Isobel Johnston the wife of an Edinburgh publisher. Scott is thought to have written the highly entertaining introduction, a dialogue between some well known epicures of the day in which they plan, with Meg's help, the formulation of the St Ronan's Culinary Club.

Meg Dods also appears in Scott's novel *St Ronan's*

Well as the capricious and eccentric landlady of the Cleikum Inn at St Ronan's near Innerleithen. This character is thought to have been modelled on Miss Marian Ritchie who was the landlady of Scott's local inn, the Cross Keys in Peebles. According to Scott, Meg was an outrageous and temperamental landlady, 'a peculiar class of wildcat' who was quite capable of turning potential guests away if she disliked the cut of their jib. Even the ones who stayed had to be prepared for her blunt, couthy Scots ways. What saved her from ruin, however, was the fact that both food and drink on her table were of the highest quality and greatly sought after.

Friar's Chicken

1½ pt chicken and/or veal stock (725 ml)
4 oz cooked chicken, finely chopped (100 g)
3 eggs
¼ pt cream (150 ml)
1 tbsp parsley, finely chopped
Salt and pepper

Put the stock into a pan and bring to the boil. Remove from the heat. Put the eggs and cream into a bowl and beat together. Add about ¼ pt (150 ml) of the hot soup gradually, beating all the time. Pass through a sieve back into the stock. Add the chicken and heat through to thicken, but do not boil or the egg will curdle. Season, add parsley and serve immediately.

It was a land of milk and honey when the Border monasteries were at the height of their wealth and power. The friars not only ate well but also possesed many 'admirable receipts in cookery'. This one was celebrated at the Cleikum Inn.

'Some like the egg curdled, and egg in great quantity, making the dish a sort of thin "ragout" of eggs and chicken.'
(Meg Dods)

BANNOCKS

At Selkirk you can buy the famous bannock in all the local bakers' shops. It is a rich, yeasted bun, shaped like a round cob loaf, both large and small, and generously filled with sultanas. When Queen Victoria was visiting Sir Walter Scott's grand-daughter at Abbotsford she is said to have refused all else to eat with her tea save a slice of the Bannock.

This is probably the best-known Scottish example of an enriched type of bread which has been preserved in its original form. Lardy Cakes are the English equivalent. In the days before raising agents, a piece of the raw bread dough was taken from the weekly batch being made and used as a foundation for a cake. Sugar, honey, spices and dried fruits were added and, of course, endless local variations developed.

Pre-18th century, these enriched breads were not available for everyday use, since fine flour and the additional ingredients were both scarce and expensive. Instead they were festive breads for such occasions as Christmas, Easter, weddings, funerals and christenings. Even as late as 1745 bakers were prohibited by law from making anything but plain bread dough except for these occasions.

Black Bun, traditionally eaten at Hogmanay, is probably the only other Scottish variation of this. It seldom appears in recipes today in its original form which had a bread dough pastry enclosing the very rich fruit and spice mixture. This in turn had a piece of dough mixed into it.

Selkirk Bannock

2 lb plain strong flour (1 kg)
4 oz lard (125 g)
4 oz butter (125 g)
¾ pt milk (400 ml)
1 oz yeast (25 g)

8 oz sugar (250 g)
1 lb sultanas or raisins or a mixture of the two (500 g)
Milk and sugar for glazing
Pinch of salt

Preheat the oven to 425°F/220°C or gas mark 7

Sift the flour into a warmed bowl, add a pinch of salt and leave in a warm place. Cream the yeast with 1 tsp of sugar. Melt the butter and lard in a pan then add the milk and allow to cool until it is just at blood heat.

Make a well in the centre of the flour and add the milk mixture and the yeast. Mix to a fairly soft dough then knead on a floured board for at least five minutes.

Put back into a floured bowl and cover with a damp cloth. Leave in a warm place till it has doubled in size. Turn the dough out onto a floured board and work in the sugar and dried fruit. Shape into four small or two large rounds. Place on a greased baking sheet and leave in a warm place till they have risen, in about 20–30 minutes. Put into a hot oven for the first 15 minutes. Reduce the heat to 375°F/190°C or gas mark 5 and bake till golden-brown, about 25–30 minutes. Large ones will take rather longer.

To glaze the tops put a little warmed milk in a cup and dissolve 1 tbsp sugar in it. Remove the bannocks about 15 minutes before they are ready and brush liberally with the glaze.

These bannocks will keep well in an airtight tin for several weeks.

Yetholm Bannock
A rich festive shortbread

5 oz butter (125 g)
2 egg yolks
2 tsp golden syrup
3 oz caster sugar (75 g)
8 oz plain flour (225 g)
$\frac{1}{4}$ tsp baking powder
1 tsp ground ginger
1 oz flaked almonds
  (25 g)
1 oz chopped mix peel
  (25 g)

Grated rind of 1 lemon
$\frac{1}{2}$ tsp vanilla essence
For the filling –
2 oz crystallised ginger,
  finely chopped (50 g)
For the topping –
1 egg yolk
1 tbsp milk
1 oz caster sugar (25 g)
1 oz flaked almonds
  (25 g)

Preheat the oven to 325°F/170°C or gas mark 3

Put the butter, yolks, golden syrup and caster sugar into a bowl and beat together till creamy. Add sifted flour, baking powder, ginger, almonds, mixed peel, lemon rind and vanilla essence. Knead all this together then divide into two equal pieces. Roll out each piece to a rectangle $\frac{1}{4}''$ thick ($\frac{1}{2}$ cm) and $6\frac{1}{2}''$ (15 cm) long by 8" (20 cm) wide. Lay one piece on a greased baking sheet and brush with egg and milk. Then sprinkle the chopped ginger evenly over the top.

    Lay the other piece on top, neaten the edges, and then brush the top of this one with egg and milk. Sprinkle evenly with flaked almonds and sugar. Bake in a cool oven for 45 minutes. Cut into fingers when cold.

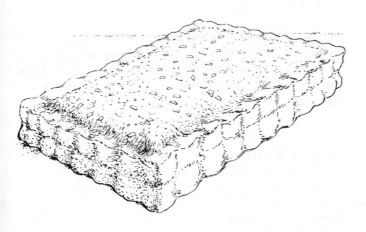

Yetholm Bannock

SOMETHING ELSE

Teviotdale or Benalty Pie

This is a batter pudding using minced beef or mutton, which makes a good high tea dish.

1 lb minced beef or lamb (500 g)	½ tsp baking powder
½ oz butter (15 g)	3 oz suet (100 g)
¼ pt water (125 ml)	1 egg
Salt and ground pepper	¼ pt milk (125 ml)
For the top –	
6 oz plain flour (200 g)	

Preheat oven to 350°F/180°C or gas mark 4

Melt the butter in a pan, add mince and break up with a fork. When all the lumps have been broken up brown well, stirring occasionally for 5 minutes. Add water and seasonings. Bring to the boil, reduce heat, cover and simmer for about 10 minutes. Put into a 2 pint (1 L) greased pie dish.

To make the top, sift the flour, baking powder and salt into a bowl. Add suet, egg and milk and mix well together. Pour this batter over the mince and bake in a moderate oven for 30–40 minutes, or until brown and firm.

Rumbledethumps

Rumbled meant 'mixed' and thumped 'bashed together', hence the unusual name for this dish. It was traditionally a main course dish in itself but can also be served as an accompaniment to roasts or stews.

1 lb potatoes, cooked and mashed (500 g)	1 medium onion, finely chopped
1 lb cabbage, cooked (500 g)	2 oz grated cheese (50 g)
2 oz butter (50 g)	Some chopped chives

Melt the butter in a large pan and add the onion. Cook gently for 5 minutes without browning. Add potatoes, chives and cabbage and mix together. Season well and put into a pie dish. Cover with cheese and brown under the grill or in the oven. Serve hot.

Soup n' Stovies

In this rich potato-growing country Stovies are very popular. Often they were made on Mondays to use up the leftovers from the weekend meat. Soup was always served as a first course. In less fortunate areas they were a

2 lb potatoes (1 kg)	Meat dripping
1 large onion, roughly chopped	Salt and pepper
Leftover roast meat cut into large chunks	

Peel potatoes and boil in salted water with the onion till they are cooked. Drain. Use the liquid for making soup.

Dry the potatoes well and then add the meat and dripping. Break up the potatoes with a wooden spoon and mix well. Season and serve.

vegetarian dish taken with a glass of chilled buttermilk. The Maris Piper variety of maincrop potato is grown and used a great deal in the Borders and is ideal for this dish with its dry floury texture. Like so many other Scottish dishes every housewife has her own Stovie recipe – this is a quick one from a Border housewife.

BAKING

Original Border Tart

For the pastry –
4 oz plain strong flour (100 g)
2½ fl oz milk (75 ml)
½ oz yeast (15 g)
1½ oz lard and margarine mixed (40 g)
Pinch of Salt
1 tsp sugar
For the custard –
1 level tbsp cornflour
½ oz butter (15 g)
¼ pt milk (150 ml)

Yolk of an egg
2 level tsp caster sugar
2 drops of vanilla essence
For the filling –
4 oz marzipan (100 g)
1 oz flaked almonds (25 g)
1 oz chopped mixed peel (25 g)
For the icing –
1 oz icing sugar (25 g)
Warm water to mix

Preheat the oven to 400°F/200°C or gas mark 6

This rich confection of marzipan, custard and almonds is encased in a yeasted pastry. When first made, the dough for the pastry would have been a piece taken from the weekly bread-making rather than made specially for the purpose. Most people today seem to prefer a much simpler version and the second recipe is from a Border housewife who has gained renown at WRI competitions for this prize-winning tart.

To make up the pastry, sieve the flour and salt into a bowl. Mix the sugar into the warm milk and crumble in the yeast. Mix in then add to the flour. Knead till smooth and put to rise in a warm place for about ¾ hr.

While this is rising you can make up the custard. Blend the cornflour with the milk, add sugar and bring to the boil. Simmer for a few minutes then remove from the heat and beat in the butter. When it has cooled a bit more, add the egg and vanilla essence. Leave to cool.

To finish the pastry and line the tin, knead the dough and roll out into a long strip. Put small pats of butter on ²/₃ of the strip. Fold up ¹/₃ and down ¹/₃ as for flaky pastry, seal edges and turn. Roll out. Repeat once, then roll out and line the tin. With leftover bits make five rounds each about the size of a 10p piece.

Roll out the marzipan to fit the base of the tart. Cover with almonds, peel and sultanas. Next spread over the custard and then place the circles of pastry on top. Cover with a piece of foil or greaseproof paper and put in a warm place for 15 minutes to prove.

Bake in a hot oven for 15–20 minutes, then reduce the heat to 375°F/190°C or gas mark 5 for another 15–20 minutes. Ice pastry circles with water icing and serve hot or cold.

Border Tart (modern version)

Twentieth-century version of a traditional confection.

For the pastry –
4 oz plain flour (100 g)
2½ oz butter (60 g)
1 oz caster sugar (25 g)
1 egg yolk
For the filling –
2 oz butter (50 g)
2 oz caster sugar (50 g)

2 eggs
1½ oz self-raising
  flour (40 g)
1 oz ground almonds
  (25 g)
2 tbsp raspberry jam
½ oz flaked almonds
  (12 g)

Preheat the oven to 350°F/180°C or gas mark 4

Make up the pastry first. Rub the fat into the flour, add sugar and make a well in the centre. Drop in the egg yolk and put your fingers into it and start bringing in the dry ingredients. It is important to keep the egg mixture together, kneading in the rest gradually, otherwise this type of pastry can be crumbly and difficult to handle. Knead with both hands to make a smooth, pliable dough which will roll out easily without cracking. The very slight heat from your hands helps to bring the dough together without 'oiling' it. Roll out and line an 8" (20 cm) fluted flan ring. Roll out the scraps to make strips for a lattice design on top.

Now make up the filling. Begin by beating the sugar and butter together till the mixture lightens in colour and becomes creamy. Add sifted flour and almonds. Spread a layer of raspberry jam in the base of the pastry and add the filling. Arrange a lattice design of pastry strips on top. Cover with some flaked almonds. Bake in a moderate oven for 25–30 minutes. About 10 minutes before it is cooked, remove from the oven and sprinkle over it a layer of icing sugar. Return to the oven. Serve with fresh cream.

Eyemouth Tart

For the pastry –
4 oz flour (100 g)
2½ oz butter (60 g)
1 oz caster sugar (25 g)
1 egg yolk
For the filling –
2 oz walnuts, chopped
 (50 g)
2 oz currants or raisins
 (50 g)

2 oz coconut (50 g)
2 oz cherries (50 g)
2 oz glacé cherries,
 chopped (50 g)
3 oz caster sugar (75 g)
2 oz melted butter (50 g)
1 egg
For the icing –
2 oz icing sugar (50 g)
Lemon juice to mix

A Border tart variation.

Preheat the oven to 375°F/190°C or gas mark 5

Begin by making up the pastry – for method see Border Tart (second recipe p. 56). Roll out and line an 8″ (20 cm) fluted flan ring.

Mix all the dry ingredients together and then add the egg and melted butter. Spread the mixture over the pastry and bake for 25 minutes in a hot oven, by when the top should be nicely browned. Mix icing sugar with enough lemon juice to make a coating icing and spread over the top while the tart is still warm. Serve cold.

BORDER SWEETIES

For some reason the Borders can lay claim to more interesting varieties of local sweeties than any other region of Scotland.

To begin with there are the round *Hawick Balls*, dark brown, tasting delicately of cinnamon blended with syrup and a subtle hint of mint. These, like many, were originally home-made, but as their fame grew so they came to be made on a larger and larger scale until today they are now a factory product obtainable in airtight tins.

Jedburgh boasts its *Jeddart Snails*. These are dark brown toffees, mildly peppermint-flavoured. The name and shape were given to them by a French prisoner-of-war in Napoleon's day when he is said to have made them for a Jedburgh baker.

Still in the heart of the Borders are the *Soor Plooms* of Peebles and Galashiels. These are round, green balls with, as their name suggests, an acid, astringent tang. The plooms are said to commemorate an incident in local history when a band of English marauders were surprised and overcome while eating unripe plums.

Coltart's Candy (pronounced *Coolter*), celebrated in the well-known children's song which Coltart wrote himself, was made in Melrose by this colourful travelling man whom the children followed around as if he were a Pied Piper. The candy was aniseed-flavoured but the recipe and custom seem to have been lost when Coltart died in 1890.

Berwick Cockles may also perhaps be included, depending on the historical moment you wish to choose for the town of Berwick-upon-Tweed. They were originally home-made, peppermint flavoured, white with pink stripes and shaped like the cockle-shells fished up near Tweedmouth harbour. They are now a commercial product as popular north of the Border as they are south of it.

Moffat Toffee is a unique toffee, hard, amber and gold striped with an intriguing tang, made in Moffat by a local family who have been making it for generations. Originally a sweetie shop product, it is now factory made with a wide distribution.

EYEMOUTH PALES

The east coast village of Eyemouth which has given its name to this method of curing fish has a picturesque sheltered harbour. The name is an apt description for a haddock smoked over sawdust to a pale golden colour, as distinct from the darker gold of the better-known Finnan Haddock.

The haddock, after splitting and brining, take only four hours in the smoke house to develop their own distinctive colour and delicate smokey flavour. The bone in this cure is not removed and this greatly enhances the flavour of the fish, though they may take a little longer to eat. Pales are best left whole and grilled, placed in the base of the grill pan with the cut side uppermost. Seasoned and liberally basted with butter during cooking, they are delicious.

March and April are the only months when haddock are not at their best.

Eyemouth Fish Pie

12 oz fresh white fish filleted (cod, haddock, whiting or sole) (350 g)
1 tbsp finely chopped shallots
½ pt milk (250 ml)
2 eggs, hard boiled
3 large tomatoes, skinned
For the sauce –
1 oz flour (25 g)
1 oz butter (25 g)
Strained cooking liquor from the fish
For the topping –
1½ lb cooked mashed potatoes (750 g)
2 oz grated cheese (50 g)
1 oz butter (25 g)
2 tbsp breadcrumbs

Put fish in a pan with milk, shallots and seasoning. Cover and simmer very gently for about 5 minutes. Cool. Make up the sauce now by melting the butter in a pan and adding the flour. Stir for a few minutes over a gentle heat without colouring. Then add the strained cooking liquor gradually and a little white wine, if available. Check seasoning and add fish and shallots. At this point slice the eggs and tomatoes. Put a layer of fish mixture, then hard-boiled eggs and tomatoes into a 2–2½ pt pie dish (1 L–1¼ L) till it is full. Beat the cheese and butter into the potatoes, check seasoning and spread on top. Sprinkle with breadcrumbs and brown under the grill.

6. Dumfries and Galloway

This corner of Scotland has its own distinctive charm as a quiet place of shapely hills, colourful villages, beautiful forests, lovely south-facing beaches and prosperous farms. All the main north-south routes bypass it, making it a more isolated area than the Borders. The busy through-route to and from Ireland, however, disrupts the peace and quiet along the main road from Dumfries to Stranraer.

GALLOWAY CATTLE

Livestock reared here on the gentle uplands have been famous for many centuries. Robert the Bruce rode a Galloway pony at Bannockburn; Shakespeare mentions Galloway nags in Henry IV; and in the 18th century Galloway cattle were walked in droves to Smithfield market in London. Today they provide prime Scots beef. Like the Aberdeen Angus breed the meat is well-distributed over the frame and is nicely marbled with fat. Where the animals are grazed on uplands for the summer months the flavour is particularly fine.

The cattle are distinguished by their thick coats which make them hardier. There is a long, silky, wavy black top-coat with a tinge of brown on the tips of the hair and, underneath, a thick mossy coat. The two are often described as a 'coat and vest'. They have no horns and are either all-black, dun or belted. The Belted Galloway breed has a white band completely encircling the body immediately behind the shoulders.

Although much of the beef is exported, it is also available in butcher's shops throughout the area, as is fine quality lamb. The uplands here are among the most heavily-stocked hill sheep-grazing areas of Scotland.

Blackface and Cheviot Sheep are the original breeds of this area. In the late 18th century they were crossed with English Border Leicesters to make a heavier sheep with more meat and better wool.

Simple methods of cooking are preferred. With such fine-quality meat there is no need to develop complicated dishes, and people prefer to roast, grill or fry the meat when they can afford it.

THE SOUTHERN UPLANDS
Separating the Central Lowlands from northern England are the wide, lonely pastoral hills known as. the Southern Uplands. They stretch across an area which divides naturally into two halves along the line of the River Annan valley which is also the major route south from Glasgow.

In the wetter western lowlands with similar climate and soil to Ayrshire, dairying naturally predominates.

In the drier, slightly more extreme climate of the eastern lowlands is the important arable area centred round the Tweed Valley. Oats, barley, wheat, potatoes and turnips are the principal crops.

The uplands in both areas are often green right over the tops, which makes them good grazing for both sheep and cattle.

Upland Lamb
You will need suitable cuts of young spring lamb. A good butcher will do most of this for you, but here are the important points in preparing the meat for roasting.
Leg on the bone: Shorten and trim the leg bone, remove the aitch bone and trim off any excess fat. **Best end:** Remove the whole chine bone, the back sinew, the tip of the blade bone and any excess fat. Trim both meat and fat from the tips of the rib bones. Score the fat

lightly in a diamond pattern. **Flank:** Bone and remove excess fat and skin. Roll up, usually with stuffing, and tie with string. **Shoulder** *(boned):* Roll up and tie with string. **Crown Roast:** Use two pieces of best end, each with six or seven cutlets. Remove the chine bone and trim the meat and fat off about ½″ (1 cm) from the end of the rib bones. Bend the cutlets round into the shape of a crown with the skin side towards the centre. Tie or sew the two pieces together. Fill the centre with stuffing. Cover the exposed ends of the bone with foil to prevent burning. **Guard of Honour:** This is easier than the crown roast, since instead of shaping the meat into a circle the two pieces of best end, after preparing in the same way for crown roast, are interlaced over the top. The centre space is then filled with stuffing. Carve each helping to serve cutlets, still crossed.

Roast Lamb

½ lb carrots, roughly chopped (225 g)	1 small onion, finely chopped
½ lb celery, roughly chopped (225 g)	1 oz cooked ham, finely chopped (25 g)
½–¾ pt stock or water (300–450 ml)	1 tbsp parsley, finely chopped
1 oz melted butter (25 g)	1 tbsp lemon thyme, finely chopped
2 oz dripping (50 g)	
For the stuffing –	Grated rind of 1 lemon
6 oz fresh breadcrumbs (175 g)	Salt and pepper
2 oz butter (50 g)	1 egg

To make up the stuffing, melt the butter and cook the onion till soft. Add to the other ingredients. Season with salt and freshly ground black pepper and bind the stuffing with egg.

To roast the meat, melt the dripping in a roasting tin and add the vegetables and seasoning. Melt the butter and spread over the meat. Set the meat on the bed of vegetables and place in a hot oven 400°F/200°C or gas mark 6 for 20–30 minutes. Reduce the heat to 325°F/170°C or gas mark 3 and baste frequently. Allow approximately 20–30 minutes per lb and another 20 minutes. Lamb is traditionally served cooked through rather than underdone. Leave to stand in a warm place before carving.

To make the gravy, pour off any surplus fat, retaining the residue. Add brown stock or water and boil up. Simmer gently to reduce the gravy, season and strain into a heated sauceboat.

Serve with redcurrant or rowan jelly (see p. 93). Very young spring lamb is served with mint jelly or sauce, boiled new potatoes and spring vegetables.

Drumlanrig Pudding

| 1½ lb rhubarb (675 g) | 8 oz sliced white bread (225 g) |
| 4–6 oz sugar (100–150 g) | 1 tsp water |

Named after Drumlanrig Castle in Dumfriesshire, a seat of the Duke of Buccleuch. It is a good variation of the English Summer Pudding.

Stew the rhubarb with water and sugar till soft. Put a layer of bread in the base of a 2 pt (1 L) pudding bowl or soufflé dish and pour some hot rhubarb on top. Add another layer of bread and more rhubarb until the dish is full, finishing with a layer of bread. Cover with a plate which just fits inside the rim of the bowl or dish. Press with a weight for at least 24 hours. To serve, loosen round the edges and turn out. Serve with soured cream and sugar.

Ecclefechan Butter Tart

For the pastry –	2 oz melted butter (50 g)
4 oz flour (100 g)	
2½ oz butter (60 g)	1 dsp wine vinegar
1 oz caster sugar (25 g)	4 oz mixed dried fruit (125 g)
1 egg yolk	
For the filling –	1 oz chopped walnuts (25 g)
1 egg	
3 oz soft brown sugar (75 g)	

This was originally made as small individual tarts, yet another variation of the Border Tart. The filling is quick to make and gives a nutty, moist-buttery result which contrasts with the crisp pastry very well.

Preheat the oven to 375°F/190°C or gas mark 5

Begin by making up the pastry – for method see Border Tart (second recipe p. 56). Roll out and line an 8″ (20 cm) fluted flan ring.

Mix the sugar, butter and eggs together then stir in the vinegar, mixed fruit and nuts. Pour into the pastry case and bake for 30 minutes. Serve hot or cold with cream.

GALLOWAY CHEESES

Dairy cattle found their way into this area quite recently compared with other livestock. It was only a hundred years ago that dairying became important in the Rhinns of Galloway and along the Solway coast. Ayrshire cattle were introduced in large numbers when the demand grew from the urban areas, and a flourishing milk, cheese, butter and cream industry developed. The main creameries are at Dumfries, Dalbeattie, Lockerbie, Stranraer and Sorbie. They ali produce mature Scottish Cheddar which is a firm-textured cheese with a full flavour. Flavours do vary according to the quality and flavour of the milk as well as the conditions throughout the process.

FISHING

Loch trout and river salmon from the Annan, Nith and Cree are an important feature of local produce in the area. Fishing in the Solway, with its swift, treacherous tides, is usually by small boat or stake nets. The major ports are at Annan, Kirkcudbright and Portpatrick.

Along the Solway coast there is a thriving fish-curing tradition. Rich supplies of salmon and the world-wide demand for smoked salmon have perhaps something to do with this. Fish-curers are often asked to cure fish which have been caught locally by visitors or by local people, and one of the most popular cures is a method using rum, honey, molasses, saltpetre and salt in the initial brining period. Latterly brown sugar is spread on the surface to give a glossy finish.

For trout, golden syrup is used instead of molasses since they tend to darken trout too much. Only the faintest trace of sweetness remains which combines well with the subtle flavour of the smoke.

Mackerel are steeped in a brine which has molasses added, then they are threaded onto rods through the heads and smoked for about six hours in a hot smoke. Oak chips from the coopers at the local whisky distillery are used as fuel with some 'green' oak sawdust as well. They are usually eaten very cold with brown bread, butter and lemon. Trout and salmon are also served very cold with a pinch of cayenne pepper, brown bread and lemon or, as appeared on a recent royal menu served in the district, 'Smoked River Nith Salmon garnished with Rothesay Shrimps'.

Solway Scallop or 'Queenie'

This scallop is distinguished by its size which is much smaller than the scallop usually found in Scottish waters. The white muscle is only about the size of a two-pence piece across but they are full of flavour and very popular. The South-West coast is the major fishing area for this Scallop in Scotland.

When they are at sea, local fishermen cook them with bacon and scrambled egg. They fry the bacon first, then cook the scallops in the fat, with perhaps a bit of butter added. They serve them with a generous helping of scrambled egg.

The eating quality is at its best through the winter from September till March.

7. The North-East

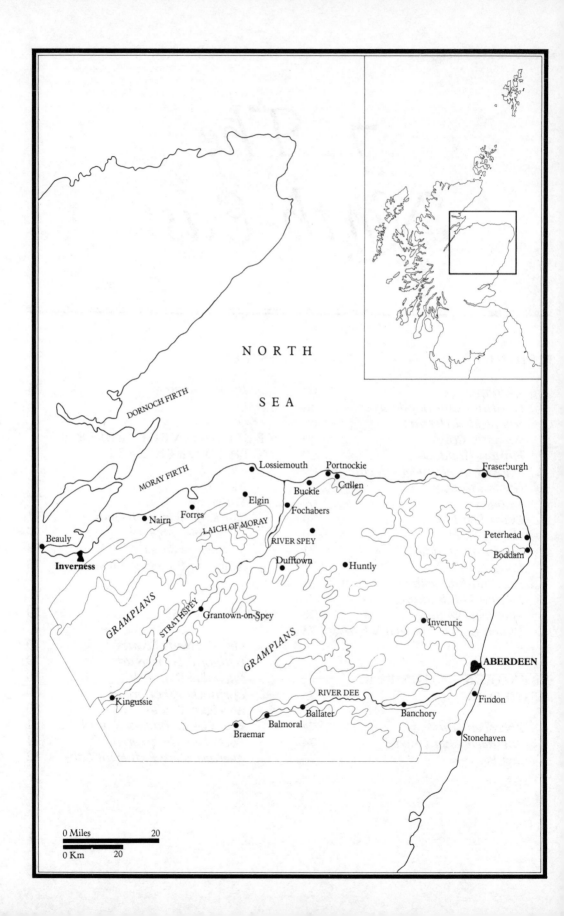

NORTH

SEA

DORNOCH FIRTH

MORAY FIRTH

Lossiemouth   Portnockie   Fraserburgh
                 Buckie   Cullen
         Elgin   Fochabers
  Forres
Nairn   LAICH OF MORAY
Beauly   RIVER SPEY   Peterhead
Inverness   Boddam
                    Dufftown   Huntly

GRAMPIANS   STRATHSPEY
         Grantown-on-Spey   Inverurie

              GRAMPIANS   ABERDEEN

                          RIVER DEE
                                                Findon
Kingussie
                      Ballater   Banchory
          Balmoral
   Braemar   Stonehaven

0 Miles   20

0 Km   20

From where the Grampian Highlands reach down almost to the sea at Stonehaven you travel along the top of rugged sea cliffs, once guarded by Dunnottar Castle, up into this distinctive area of coastal lowlands. Behind are the red sandstone soils of Angus and beyond is the grey granite country of Aberdeenshire.

Despite a rather bleak climate and soil won from a 'rubbish dump' of the Ice Age the North-Eastern lowlands today are one of the best-farmed areas of Scotland. The 18th-century Improving Lairds started the work of attacking the wilderness of moors and mosses where previously farmers had merely scraped a living from an unfriendly stony soil. They enclosed fields, drained land and the people were set to work clearing the stones which they made into dry-stone dykes (walls).

Although this is north of the Highland line, people here dislike being regarded as Highlanders. Highlanders, to them, are the Celtic peoples who live on the Atlantic coast by the mild airs and copious warm rain of the Gulf Stream. In the North-East their racial background has links with the Scandinavians, the Dutch and other people of the European continent; their climate, similar to these peoples, is one of dry winds and cold currents coming from the vast sub-Arctic plains of the North and East. Geography and race have probably both combined to make the north-easterners different, not just in language, but also in their habits of thought, manners, and, most of all in their attitude to life and work.

FISHING

This is the traditional centre of the Scottish fishing industry with Aberdeen, Fraserburgh and Peterhead the major fishing ports. The main reasons for the growth of high-technology fishing in this area are the nearness to the North Sea fishing grounds, a wealth of natural harbours round the coast and better land communications with the South than the fishing ports on the West Coast enjoy.

The fishing industry has experienced and still undergoes periods of change. But probably the most outstanding change took place during the latter part of the 19th century when there was a major revolution in the habits of fish consumption. Transportation had always been the main problem with such a perishable commodity. Also, the landlords owned the rivers and lochs and often demanded a share or all of the catch, so that

freshwater fish was not always very plentiful. Sea fish
was more available, but although the catches might be
large, slow boats and bad roads meant that only people
on or near the coast enjoyed it in its fresh state. Even
today people of the fishing ports and harbours have a
keen nose and palate for freshness and will reject as
'rotten', fish which would be quite acceptable to an
inland consumer.

Speldings

In the North-East excess fish supplies were often carried inland by the fisher women in wicker *crees* which
they carried on their backs, walking far into the countryside. They exchanged the fish for money or more
usually for eggs, butter, chickens, oatmeal or cheese.
Even this did not deal with all the surplus fish and much
of it was salted and dried. A cure for the surplus haddock was known as Speldings. The fish were gutted and
split with the heads left on, then soaked in strong brine
and laid on smooth pebbles on the beach during the
day. If it rained they had to be brought in. After a few
days, as they hardened, they were pressed with more
flat stones. The drying process took about a week,
depending on the size of the fish, and at the end of it
they were a greenish-red colour and quite hard.

Findrums and Boddams

The fisher women, since they were the curers as well as
the sellers, hung some of the pressed fish up the chimney and smoked them over the peat fire. This smoked
Spelding was known as a Findrum or Boddam Cure.
Findrum after the fishing village of Findon six miles
south of Aberdeen, and *Boddams* after the fishing village near Peterhead. These are thought to be the cures
from which the Finnan Haddock developed. The Speldings, Findrums and Boddams were now easily transported and found their way as far South as London.

Salt-pickled Herring

The other major type of curing developed on this coast
prior to the revolution in fish consumption was salt-
pickled herring. It was a process perfected by the Dutch
in the late 14th and early 15th century, and Dutch curers
came to Aberdeenshire to show the fisher women the
method. The English term derives, in fact, from Dutch
Peeckle-Herring.

The fresh herring were first *gibbed* to remove the

gills and the long gut, leaving the roe and milt and the rest of the viscera which contribute to its characteristic flavour. Then rows of them were packed in layers with coarse salt between, the herring lying slightly on its side with its back uppermost and the next layer lying in the opposite direction. When the barrel was full the lid was put on to exclude the air, then the fish left to settle for a few days when another layer could be added before finally the coopers closed up the barrel.

Filleting the fish and packing the barrel was a skilled job for fisher women and girls, some of whom travelled around the country following the herring landings. The fishing villages of Fraserburgh, Peterhead and Buckie grew and flourished into towns from the sale of salt herring, both to the home market and to several countries in Central Europe.

The change in fish-eating habits started with the railways, was further encouraged by the use of ice and refrigeration, and then by steam trawling – all of which took place in the 19th century. Now it was no longer necessary to create a non-perishable commodity. But instead of abandoning old traditions, curers began to develop and modify to make the fish more palatable. At this point the kipper was developed in the North-East of England, and in Scotland the Finnan.

Whitefish Cures

Today the **Finnan Haddock** is made with a medium-sized haddock, gutted and cleaned, then split open with the backbone on the right in the Aberdeen cure. The fish are then brined and cold-smoked till they are a pale straw colour for three to four hours, depending on the size of the fish. Several variations of this cure are available today. Similar in every way to the Finnan, except that they are brined and smoked for a shorter time, are the Eyemouth (see p. 59) and Glasgow Pales.

Smoked Fillet or **Aberdeen Fillet** is a single fillet with the skin on, taken from medium and large haddock. They are brined and cold-smoked for a shorter period than the whole fish. **Golden Cutlets** are filleted haddock or whiting without the skin which are very lightly brined and dyed, then cold-smoked. Because the skin and bones have been removed a lot of the flavour is lost. **Smokies** are the only variation of this cure which are hot-smoked till they are cooked through. As they are not opened up, they have retained the original name of *closefish* (see p. 30). Of the processed whitefish today, the haddock smoked cures dominate the market. Some saith, whiting, cod, ling and sole are also smoked, but not in such large quantities as haddock. Traditionally this was the coastline where whitefish cures reached perfection. Herring cures are also to be found here, but it was originally from the West Coast that the herrings' fame travelled far and wide as a Loch Fyne Kipper (see p. 87).

Dried Salt Fish

Cod and Ling are the only fish which are still salted and dried till rock-hard. People in the North-East and other parts of Scotland hung them from a rafter in the kitchen and they were used when other food was scarce. The fish was soaked then boiled and mixed with mashed potatoes. The flakes of the fish break up into very fine hairs and because of this they were known as Hairy Tatties. An example of Aberdeenshire's Scandinavian links is the close resemblance between Hairy Tatties and Norwegian *Lutefish* which is eaten with boiled potatoes and stewed yellow peas.

Cullen Skink

1 large Finnan Haddock or 8 oz fillet (250 g)	2 pts water (1 L)
1 medium onion, roughly chopped	$\frac{1}{2}$ pt milk (250 ml)
	2 oz butter (50 g)
Salt and pepper	1 lb potatoes (500 g)

Garnish –
Chopped parsley
4 tbsp single cream

Put fish, onion, seasoning and water into a large pan and bring to the boil. Cover and simmer for 20 minutes. Meanwhile peel, boil and mash potatoes.

Lift out fish, leave to cool for a minute and take off all skin and bone. Strain the stock and return to the pan. Add flaked fish, milk, butter and potato. Bring to the boil and simmer for a few minutes. Correct seasoning and serve garnished with a little chopped parsley and a spoonful of cream per person.

Fisher people belong to close-knit communities, depending on one another for support in their precarious occupation, and their villages are always quite distinctive and separate from other habitation. Along this coastland some of the fishing villages are perched on top of cliffs, some sheltered at the bottom, others standing on the edge of the beach and some like Cullen, a district within a town known as the Seatown. The soup-stew which originated here, but is typical of fisher food all round the coast, is traditionally made with the whole unboned Finnan which undoubtedly makes the best soup since the bones and skin have so much of the flavour. It can be made with fillet of smoked fish, but it will not taste the same. Skink was an old Scots word for 'soup' or 'broth'.

Ham and Haddie

2 Finnan Haddock	1 oz butter (25 g)
½ lb bacon (250 g)	Salt and pepper

Grease the grill pan with butter. Place in fish, flesh side uppermost. Dot with butter or brush with melted butter. Season with salt and pepper. Put on grill to heat. Lay bacon on top of grid and place on top of grill pan. Place under the grill and cook, turning once. Remove bacon and grid and keep the bacon warm. Finish off cooking the Finnans – about another 5 minutes. Lift out of the pan onto a heated serving plate. Put the bacon on top and pour over the pan juices. Sometimes this is served with a tbsp of cream.

Bacon rather than pork seems to have been preferred in this area and there is now an important pig-processing industry here. The use of the term ham *in Scotland loosely refers to any kind of bacon and not merely the cured leg joint and cooked meat from it which is the usual English interpretation of the word. In Scotland this is usually called* cooked ham.

The traditional method is to fry these two together but this grilling method prevents the fish drying out and preserves all the juices and flavour at the same time.

Fisherman's Stew

1 oz butter (25 g)	1½ lb filleted white
6 slices of streaky bacon	fish (¾ kg)
3 large onions	1 pt milk (500 ml)
2 lb potatoes (1 kg)	
Salt and freshly ground black pepper	

Melt the butter in a large pan. Meanwhile chop up the bacon roughly and then fry gently in the butter. Now chop up the onions finely and add to the bacon. Mix well, cover and leave to cook very gently for about 5 minutes till the onions are soft but not browned.

Slice the potatoes about ¼″ thick (½ cm) and add to the pot. Mix everything together, cover and cook gently for another five minutes. Season with salt and black pepper. Add water and bring slowly to simmering point. Chop up the fish roughly into 2″ pieces (5 cm) and place on top. Cover and simmer very gently till the potatoes are cooked – about 20 to 30 minutes.

Check seasoning and serve in deep soup plates. Milk and/or butter can be added if you want to make this into a thick, substantial soup.

This is the sort of soup-stew made and eaten at sea with some of the filleted fresh catch. It is served up steaming hot in pint mugs and is really a fisherman's version of Stovies.

Fish Pudding with breadcrumbs

1 lb Aberdeen fillet (500 g)	1 oz butter (25 g)
	1 tbsp chopped parsley
¼ pt milk (150 ml)	Salt and pepper
2 eggs	
2 oz fine white breadcrumbs (50 g)	

Fish pudding recipes with either breadcrumbs or potatoes are many and varied in this area. There was always one day of the week when they were made, principally for the children,

*who disliked picking bones out
of fish.*

Preheat the oven to 350°F/180°C or gas mark 4

Put the fish into a pan and cover with milk. Bring to
the boil, cover and simmer for about 5–10 minutes.
Remove fish and flake into a bowl. Add 1½ oz of the
breadcrumbs, yolks of eggs, parsley, salt and pepper
and butter melted in the milk that the fish was cooked
in. Mix thoroughly.

Beat up the whites till stiff and fold into the mixture.
Put into a greased 2 pt (1 L) soufflé dish and sprinkle
with the remaining breadcrumbs. Bake in a moderate
oven for 35–40 mins. Serve immediately.

Findon Fish Pudding

*This recipe was found written
on a piece of paper among the
pages of an old cookery book
from this area. It was described
at the end as 'very convenient'.*

2 lb potatoes (1 kg)	2 tbsp milk or cream
1¼ lb Aberdeen fillet	*For the top –*
(625 g)	1 tomato
1 oz butter (25 g)	1 oz grated cheese (25 g)

Preheat the oven to 350°F/180°C or gas mark 4

Peel the potatoes and put on to boil. While they are
boiling put the fish onto a greased baking tray, dot with
butter and sprinkle with milk. Cover with a piece of
paper or foil and bake for 20 minutes. Remove from the
oven and leave to cool.

The potatoes can now be drained and mashed. Drain
the cooking liquor from the fish into the potatoes, then
flake the fish in on top. Mash all this together and season
well. Put into a greased 2½ pt (1¼ L) pie dish. Put sliced
tomato on top and cover with grated cheese. Heat
through in the oven and serve with leeks in a cream
sauce.

Aberdeen Whiting

*This is a popular way of
cooking whiting when very
fresh.*

8 small whiting, whole	¼ pt fish stock or
Seasoned flour	milk (125 ml)
2 oz butter (50 g)	2 tbsp cream
Chopped parsley	
Chopped chives or shallots	

Clean and gut the fish. Flour them and fry in butter
slowly without browning. Chop up the parsley and
chives very finely. Add to stock or milk and cream, mix
well and pour over the whiting before they are cooked.
Serve the fish and sauce with boiled potatoes.

Blawn or Wind-Blown Whiting

6 whiting (line-caught and very fresh)	Salt
	Butter

Clean and wipe whiting, take out the eyes. Cover the fish with salt and then remove them immediately, shaking off the surplus salt. Pass a string through the eye holes and hang them up to dry where there is a good current of dry air. Remove them the next day if they are small, or leave for 3 days if they are large.

To cook them, brush with melted butter and grill on both sides. Serve with oatcakes and a pat of butter on each one.

This is an old fisher way with white fish, particularly whiting. After salting briefly, the fish are hung up on pegs at the side of the house out of the sun and left overnight to sharpen the flavour. They are then cooked simply with butter, needing no other sauce.

ABERDEEN ANGUS BEEF AND PORK

Cattle-rearing has always been the most important farming activity in the North-East. But since there was not enough grass to keep them alive during the long, cold winter most cattle had to be either killed in the autumn and salted, or driven south to the Falkirk tryst and sold to North of England farmers. The turnip changed all this. It was an ideal crop for soil and climate; and it provided enough winter-feeding for the cattle. As in all other livestock areas the turnip meant that Aberdeenshire farmers could now interest themselves in breeding good stock.

The history of pedigree-breeding in this area is a complicated tale, but there has obviously been much interchange of stock with the neighbouring areas of Kincardine and Angus, as well as further afield. This eventually produced the well-known Aberdeen Angus and Scottish Shorthorn breeds. These cattle, being docile, healthy, and well adapted to a variety of climates, mature early and give a very fine beef. It is not surprising that they are now to be found in many other countries throughout the world as well as in other parts of Britain. In this predominantly livestock area pigs and poultry are farmed, as well as sheep-grazing on the upland pastures.

In comparison with the selection of regional fish recipes the meat ones are limited. The reasons for this are the same as in any other stock-rearing area of Scotland where the people could not afford to eat their most valuable asset. If any of them did, then the methods used were of the simplest, the fine quality of the meat requiring no elaboration (see p. 22).

This is an old farmhouse recipe which originally used up the end of the ham. The addition of pork makes it moister, but this is not essential and 1 lb (500 g) of steak mince can be used instead. A good butcher will usually be prepared to mince the pork for you provided he is able to put about ½ lb (225 g) of steak mince through afterwards to clean out the pork which, luckily, is just what you need for this recipe.

Aberdeen Sausage

½ lb minced stewing steak (250 g)	6 fresh sage leaves, finely chopped
½ lb minced lean shoulder of pork (250 g)	¼ nutmeg, grated
1 lb minced streaky bacon (500 g)	2 eggs
4 oz fine white bread-crumbs or rolled oats (125 g)	Salt and freshly ground black pepper

Preheat the oven to 350°F/180°C or gas mark 4

Put all the ingredients into a bowl and mix them together. Leave in a cool place for about three hours.

For the steaming method, mould the mixture into a sausage shape and wrap in greased foil or greaseproof paper. Put on a large pan of boiling water and immerse a large piece of cotton or linen cloth in it. Remove from the pan, lay it out on a table and wrap up the sausage, tying it at the ends. Put a plate in the base of the pan and lower in the sausage. Have the water almost covering it and simmer gently with the lid on for 3 hours. When cooked, remove cloth and foil and roll in browned crumbs while still hot. Serve hot or cold.

For the baking method, press the mixture into a greased 3 pt (1½ L) ovenproof dish, cover with a buttered paper and then foil or a lid. Place in a tray of water, about 1" (2.5 cm) deep and bake in a moderate oven for 1½–2 hours. Serve hot or cold.

Fine quality meat can be cooked to perfection by the simplest methods. This sort of recipe, however, is a 20th century development which extends the repertoire of traditional Scottish dishes while at the same time utilising other excellent local produce.

Aberdeen Angus Steak

4×4–6 oz entrecôte or fillet steak (125–175 g)	8 fl. oz red wine (250 ml)
1½ oz butter (40 g)	3 tbsp double cream
2 tbsp oil	Salt and pepper
1 oz medium oatmeal (25 g)	2 tbsp whisky
1 small onion, very finely chopped	

Melt the butter in a large frying pan and cook the oatmeal slowly till it has browned slightly. Remove this from the pan. Put in a tbsp of oil and add the onions. Cook them till they are also lightly browned. Remove and put in a warm place with the oatmeal. Now add another tbsp of oil and fry the steak on both sides till cooked. Remove and put in a warm place.

To finish the dish add the red wine and scrape round the pan to mix in with the pan juices. Simmer gently for a few minutes to reduce it and concentrate the flavour. Add the cream, onions and oatmeal. Season and adjust the consistency with a little more wine if necessary. Return the steaks to the pan. Pour over the whisky and flame. Serve immediately.

Sea Pie

For the filling –
1½ lb stewing steak
  (¾ kg)
1 carrot, diced
1 medium onion, finely
  chopped
1 small piece of turnip,
  diced
Cold water
1 tbsp plain flour

Salt and pepper
1 tbsp oil for frying
For the pastry –
8 oz self-raising flour
  (250 g)
4 oz suet, finely
  chopped (125 g)
¼ pt water *(approx.)*
  (150 ml)
Salt and pepper

The connection this pie has with the sea is obscure, unless of course it was originally made and eaten at sea. Whatever its origins, made with prime beef of the area, it is an excellent way of using the tougher cuts. The suet pastry is softer and doughier if the pie is cooked in a pot. In the oven it is crisper, but both ways are excellent.

Preheat the oven to 350°F/180°C or gas mark 4

Put the oil into the pan or casserole, add the onion and brown. Cut the steak up into small pieces and add. Cook till browned. Now add the carrot and turnip and season with salt and pepper. Just cover the meat with cold water, bring to the boil and simmer for about 1 hour with the lid on or bake in a moderate oven. Just before adding the pastry top, sprinkle and stir in the flour.

Make up the pastry just before it is required. Sift the flour into a bowl and add the suet, salt and pepper. If the suet is frozen it is much easier to chop up finely. Mix in the water to make a fairly stiff elastic dough. Roll out the size of the pot or casserole and place on top of the meat. Cover with the lid and cook for another 20–30 minutes. If the pie is in the oven the lid can be left off and the pastry browned on top.

SWEET

Burnt Cream

4 eggs
½ pt milk (300 ml)
½ pt single or double
  cream (300 ml)

2 oz caster sugar
  (50 g)

A nineteenth-century recipe which came from a country house in Aberdeenshire. Originally the custard was cooked in a pan rather than in the oven. Other recipes flavour the cream with a stick of cinnamon and some zest of orange. The sugar in this recipe is burnt on top, rather than mixed through the custard, to make a crisp crust which contrasts with the creamy texture of the custard. It is essential to use cream for at least half the quantity since the flavour of the custard depends so much on it.

Preheat the oven to 350°F/180°C or gas mark 4

Heat the cream and milk to blood heat. Beat the eggs in a bowl and pour in the heated milk and cream, beating well.

Strain into a greased 2 pt (1 L) pie dish put into a dish with about 2" (5 cm) of water and bake for 35 minutes in a moderate oven. When set, remove from the oven and cover the top with a thick layer of caster sugar and brown under a hot grill. The sugar should form a brown crust about 1/8" (3 mm) thick.

FRUIT AND VEGETABLES IN THE NORTH-EAST

Along the coastal lowlands of the Moray Firth is the fertile, low-lying area known as the Laich of Moray. Here the climate is a good deal warmer than out in Buchan and also there are deposits of the very valuable red sandstone soils so useful for arable farming. Moray has the highest percentage of woodland in Britain for its area, with Nairn a close second. Conifers predominate – Scots pine, spruce, larch and also the Corsican pines of Culbin. Sheltered by the forest, vegetables, soft fruits, apples and pears mature and ripen well here.

The turnips (neeps) in this soup are the large yellow ones, available through the winter months, known south of the Border as swedes, rather than the smaller white variety which in Scotland are known as new turnips.

Turnips were often used for making brose in this area. This was a custom which used the water that vegetables had been cooked in – nothing was ever thrown away. Some of the vegetable water was poured over oatmeal in a bowl to make a thick porridge consistency and this was eaten with the puréed vegetables.

Neep Bree

1½ lb turnips (¾ kg)	½ pt milk (250 ml)
1 medium onion, finely chopped	Pinch of ginger
	Salt and pepper
2 oz butter (50 g)	

Garnish –
Chopped chives and 1 tbsp cream per person

Peel and chop the turnip roughly and blanch in boiling water for 2–3 minutes. Pour off water. Melt butter in a large pot and add onions and turnip. Season with salt and pepper and add ginger. Cover and cook very gently for about 10 minutes, stirring occasionally.

Add the water, bring to the boil and simmer gently for 30–40 minutes when the turnip should be tender. Liquidise till it is a very fine purée or pass twice through a fine sieve.

Correct the consistency with a little milk if it is too thick and check seasoning. Serve hot, garnished with chopped chives and a tbsp of cream in each bowl.

Kailkenny

1 lb cabbage, cooked
(500 g)
1 lb potatoes, cooked
(500 g)

2 tbsp cream
Salt and freshly ground
black pepper

This is another vegetable dish of the area, made by mashing equal quantities of cooked potatoes and cooked cabbage then stirring in some cream.

Mash cabbage and potatoes together. Stir in cream, season with pepper and salt. Mix thoroughly and serve very hot.

Skirlie or Skirl-in-the-pan

2 oz suet (50 g)
1–2 medium onions,
finely chopped

6 oz medium oatmeal
(175 g)
Salt and pepper

This was originally a cheap, sustaining meal served with Chappit Tatties and a glass of milk. It was often a Saturday dish when mothers had a day off. It makes a good stuffing for chicken and also is often served as an accompaniment to game birds or roast meats. Sometimes water is added and there is a great variety in the type of fat used. In this area they favour beef or mutton suet. Skirl means 'loud noise'.

Chop the suet finely and put into a heated frying pan. When it is thoroughly melted, add onions and brown them well. Add enough oatmeal to absorb the fat and make a fairly thick mixture. Season well and cook for a few minutes. Serve with meat or game either roasted or stewed.

Morayshire Apples

1 lb cooking apples
(500 g)
$\frac{1}{2}$ gill water (75 ml)
3 oz granulated sugar
(75 g)
4 cloves
For the topping –
2 oz fresh beef suet
(50 g)

4 oz soft brown sugar
(125 g)
4 oz medium oatmeal
(125 g)
1 oz hazel nuts, finely
chopped (25 g)

This is a good winter pudding. The topping is a kind of sweet skirlie mixture with nuts.

Preheat the oven to 350°F/180°C or gas mark 4

Bring the water to the boil and add the cloves. Cover and leave for 10 minutes. Add sugar and boil up to dissolve. While waiting for this to infuse, make up the top. Chop the suet up finely and mix with half of the brown sugar, oatmeal and hazel nuts. Peel, core and slice the apples and place in a 2$\frac{1}{2}$pt (1$\frac{1}{4}$L) pie dish. Strain the infused syrup over the apples.

Cover the apples with the topping mixture spread evenly, and lastly sprinkle over it the other 2 oz (50 g) of brown sugar. Press down and bake in a moderate oven for 1 hour. Serve hot with whipped cream.

Strawberry Sweet

A delicious summer sweet when strawberries and redcurrants are plentiful.

1 lb strawberries (500 g)
1 lb red currants (500 g)

1 lb caster sugar (500 g)
¼ pt whipping cream (125 ml)

Spread out the strawberries on a large plate and sprinkle over them half of the sugar. Leave in a cool place overnight. Next day put the redcurrants into a pan with a little water and cook gently till they are soft. Strain off juice and add the other half of the sugar to it. Put in a pan and bring to the boil. Boil for 10–15 minutes until you have a thick syrup. Add the strawberries and their syrup to the hot syrup and leave to cool. Before serving pour into individual dishes, chill and top with some whipped cream.

Aberdeen Preserved Apples

This preserving recipe is a good way of keeping some of the autumn apples for a few months. The original recipe used Ribston Pippins, but Cox's Pippins are also suitable, or any other hard variety.

2 lb hard eating apples (1 kg)
2 lb white sugar (1 kg)
4 oz whole fresh ginger root (125 g)

4 pt water (2 L)
2 pt buttermilk (1 L)

Peel and core the apples and put them into a deep bowl. Cover with buttermilk and put a plate on top to keep them fully submerged. Leave for 48 hours.

Peel the ginger root and cut up roughly into chunks. Put into a pan with the water. Bring to the boil, cover and simmer till it is soft, about 15 minutes. Add sugar, stir to dissolve and bring to the boil. Simmer for another 15 minutes. Leave to cool.

Remove the apples from the buttermilk (it can still be used for baking) and rinse them in cold water. Put the apples into the pan with the cold syrup and heat gently till they are just simmering. Cook till the apples are just soft and have become clear.

Lift out the apples and place in a large jar, cover with syrup and the ginger. They will keep well for several months. Serve the apples and the now-crystallised ginger with cream.

BAKING

Rural areas, where bakers' shops are not just around the corner, have a tendency to produce more regional baking specialities than urban ones. Perhaps it is because people know one another better and there is a great deal more visiting, tea-drinking and sampling of home-made recipes. Whatever the reason, the home-baking tradition is strong in this area, with many distinctive qualities.

Mrs MacNab's Scones

1 lb self-raising flour* (450 g)	2 oz butter (50 g)
	1 egg
1 tsp salt	¾ pint milk (400 ml)

Preheat the oven to 425°F/220°C or gas mark 7

(*Use buttermilk and plain flour with 1 heaped tsp cream of tartar and 1 heaped tsp bicarbonate of soda for a sharper-tasting, moister scone.)

Sift the flour and salt twice. Rub in the butter. Make a well in the centre and add the egg and milk. Mix to a soft, elastic dough. Turn out onto a floured board and dust with flour. Flour your hands well and break off small pieces. Flour them well and make into balls, handling as lightly and as little as possible. Put onto the greased baking sheet and press down lightly on top. Bake in a very hot oven for 8–10 minutes.

Mrs MacNab was a 19th-century Ballater farmer's wife who became famous both for her fine baking and for the royal visitors who came to sample it. Of all the cakes and buns which she made it was a simple but perfect scone which attracted Queen Victoria and her guests. Lightness in handling and speed in making are the secrets of producing a good scone.

Balmoral Shortbread

12 oz plain flour (375 g)	4 oz sugar (125 g)
8 oz butter (225 g)	Pinch of salt

Preheat the oven to 350°F/180°C or gas mark 4

Makes 36

Sift the flour onto a board. Put the sugar into a separate pile and, using both hands, work all the sugar into the butter. Now start kneading in the flour a little at a time. When all the flour is worked in you should have a firm ball of dough. Sprinkle a little flour on the board and roll out very thinly to between ⅛″–¼″ (3–5 mm). Cut into circles about 2½″ in diameter (6½ cm) and prick with a fork in domino fashion with three pricks.

Bake on a greased tray in a moderate oven for 30 minutes.

This is the country of Royal Deeside, probably the most heavily-trodden tourist trail outside Edinburgh. Queen Victoria was very fond of this shortbread and is said to have enjoyed a piece regularly with her afternoon tea. Her restrained taste for the plain and simple delicacies of the Scottish baking tradition contrasts interestingly with the more exuberant ornamentation which we usually associate with things Victorian.

Pitcaithly Bannock

A rich festive shortbread made into a thick, round bannock.

8 oz plain flour (225 g)	8 oz butter (225 g)
4 oz cornflour (100 g)	2 oz flaked almonds
2 oz icing sugar (50 g)	(50 g)
2 oz caster sugar (50 g)	Citron peel

Preheat the oven to 325°F/170°C or gas mark 3

Sift the flours and sugars onto a board and knead into the butter gradually. This is the traditional method which takes a little longer than the creaming method.

If you use the creaming method, just beat the sugar and butter together till creamy then add the flour and mix in. Add almost all the almonds to the mixture and roll out into one large round about ¾″ (2 cm) thick or two smaller ones. Sprinkle some flaked almonds and some citron peel on top and press them in by rolling over gently with a rolling pin. Now decorate the edge by pinching with finger and thumb.

Put on a greased baking sheet and bake for ¾–1 hour in a slow oven. If you have made two smaller ones they will not take quite so long. They should be a pale golden colour.

Portnockie Shortbread

One of the few shortbread recipes which uses margarine and butter. The flavour is not so rich, but nevertheless it is a very good shortbread.

12 oz plain flour (350 g)	4 oz butter (125 g)
5 oz rice flour (150 g)	5 oz sugar (150 g)
8 oz margarine (250 g)	

Preheat the oven to 350°F/180°C or gas mark 4

Measure the flours and sugar onto a board. Knead gradually into the butter and margarine until you have a fairly firm ball of dough. Roll out to $^1/_8$″ thick (½ cm) and cut into rounds. Bake in a moderate oven for 15–20 minutes. Dust with a little caster sugar.

Aberdeen Crulla

These are plaited doughnuts. Their name is possibly derived from the Dutch word krullen, *meaning a curl or a scroll, which would certainly apply to the shape. Crullers are popular in America and are thought to have been introduced by Dutch settlers. The Dutch connection*

2 oz butter (50 g)	7 oz self-raising flour
2 oz sugar (50 g)	(200 g)
1 egg	Oil for deep frying

Warm the butter and sugar in a bowl and then beat till they become lighter and creamier. Beat in the egg. Stir in the flour to make a fairly stiff dough. Turn out onto a floured board and knead till smooth; divide into 6–8 pieces and roll into thick sausages about 3″ long (7½ cm). Cut into three strips but leave them joined at one end. Now plait the strips. Seal the end with a little water and deep-fry, turning once till they are golden brown. Dust with caster sugar and serve hot as a sweet or cold as teabread.

with this area of Scotland was also very strong at one time.

Butteries or Buttery Rowies

2 lb strong white flour (1 kg)
1 oz yeast (25 g)
1 tsp sugar
1 pt lukewarm water (600 ml)

1 level tbsp salt
12 oz lard (325 g)
12 oz butter (325 g)

Preheat the oven to 400°F/200°C or gas mark 6

Warm the flour and salt in a bowl. Blend the yeast and sugar together until the yeast becomes liquid. Add some of the lukewarm water. Make a well in the centre of the flour and add most of the water. Keep a little back since you may not need it all. Some flours absorb more liquid than others so it is difficult to be exact. The dough should be quite firm yet not too stiff when you have finished kneading it. Put in a floured bowl, cover with a damp cloth and leave in a warm place till it has doubled in size.

When it is ready, knock down the dough and knead for a few minutes. Then roll out into a large rectangle and divide into thirds. Place ¹/₃ of the fat on the top ²/₃ (as for flaky pastry) fold up the bottom ¹/₃ and fold down the top ¹/₃. Seal the edges, turn and roll out.

Rest the dough in a cool place for 10 minutes then continue in the same way, with a rest between rollings to allow the dough to relax. After the final rolling, roll the dough out to about ½″ (1 cm) thick.

Cut the dough roughly into squares and shape these into oval bun shapes, turning in the edges. Put on a greased, floured tin with some space between them and put in a warm place to prove for about 30 minutes till they are risen nicely. Bake in a fairly hot oven for 15–20 minutes.

This rich type of bread roll is to be found in all bakers' shops in this area and is one of their most distinctive baking specialities. Butter and lard are layered through the bread dough to give it a flaky result rather like a French croissant The Buttery shape is less sophisticated, however, since it is made into roughly-shaped ovals. They are eaten warm, usually for breakfast, spread with butter and marmalade.

Fochabers Gingerbread

4 oz butter (125 g)
2 oz sugar (50 g)
4 oz treacle (125 g)
1 egg
2 oz currants (50 g)
2 oz sultanas (50 g)
1½ oz candied peel (65 g)
½ lb flour (250 g)

1 heaped tsp each of ginger, mixed spice and cinnamon
1 level tsp ground cloves
1 tsp bicarbonate of soda
¼ pt beer (125 ml)

A delicious rich, fruity gingerbread which is mixed with beer.

81

Preheat the oven to 350°F/180°C or gas mark 4

Put the butter and sugar into a bowl, warm slightly in the oven, and then beat till the mixture lightens in colour and becomes creamy.

Remove the lid of the treacle tin and place the tin either over a low heat or in a warm place to melt it slightly. Place the tin on the scales to check the weight then pour 4 oz (125 g) into the mixture. Add the egg and beat in. Add the dried fruit and peel and sift in the flour and spices. Dissolve the soda in beer and add. Mix all the ingredients thoroughly together and put into a 1 lb (½ kg) size loaf tin which has been lined with grease-proof paper.

Bake in a moderate oven for 1 hour.

Aberdeenshire Rich Fruit Cake

An Aberdeenshire master-baker made this cake for weddings, christenings and other celebrations. It is richly flavoured with rum and cinnamon, which gives it a distinctive flavour quite unlike any other rich fruit cakes of this type. It has to mature for at least a month before use, to allow the flavours to develop and the rum to penetrate through the cake.

½ lb butter (250 g)
½ lb caster sugar (250 g)
12 oz self-raising flour (350 g)
4–5 eggs
1¼ lb currants (625 g)
4 oz sultanas (125 g)
½ lb mixed peel, finely chopped (250 g)
4 oz glacé cherries, finely chopped (125 g)
½ oz cinnamon (15 g)
2–3 fl oz rum for mixing (50–75 ml)
2–3 fl oz rum for soaking (50–75 ml)

Preheat the oven to 325°F/170°C or gas mark 3

Warm the butter and sugar in a large bowl. Break the eggs into another bowl, beat and warm so that they are the same temperature as the sugar and butter. This is important since the fat is much less likely to separate and curdle if the eggs are also warm when they are added. To mix, beat the sugar and butter till they become light and creamy. Add the warmed egg gradually and beat in. Sift the flour and cinnamon and stir in gently. Add the currants, sultanas, peel and cherries and fold in. Mix to a fairly stiff consistency with rum. Put into a lined 9" (23 cm) round cake tin, level the top and bake for about three hours. To test – put in a skewer and if ready it should come out clean. When cool soak the base with rum. Decorate with marzipan and icing.

8. The Highlands and Inner Hebrides

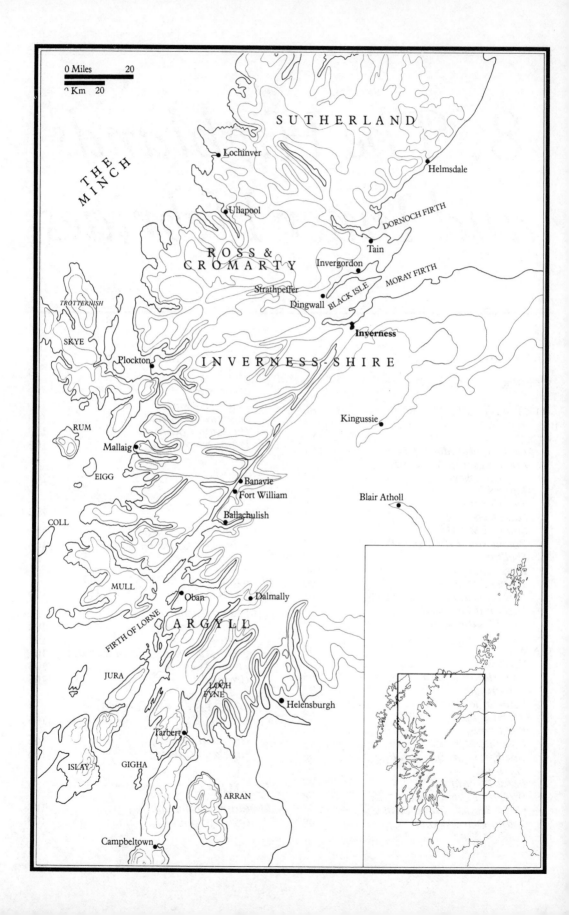

0 Miles 20

Km 20

THE MINCH

SUTHERLAND

Lochinver

Helmsdale

Ullapool

DORNOCH FIRTH

ROSS &
CROMARTY

Tain

Invergordon

TROTTERNISH

Strathpeffer

MORAY FIRTH

Dingwall BLACK ISLE

SKYE

Inverness

Plockton

INVERNESS-SHIRE

Kingussie

RUM

Mallaig

EIGG

COLL

Banavie

Fort William

Blair Atholl

Ballachulish

MULL

Oban

Dalmally

FIRTH OF LORNE

ARGYLL

JURA

LOCH
FYNE

Helensburgh

Tarbert

ISLAY

GIGHA

ARRAN

Campbeltown

Mountains and moorland dominate this desolate and spectacular country. Although the region covers about half the total area of the country, only five per cent of the population lives here.

CROFTING COUNTRY

Along the shores of the sea lochs, which cut everywhere into the rugged northern and western coast, in the glens and on the many islands, the crofting system prevails. An ancient system of hereditary tenure of small patches of cultivated land, combined with rights of common grazing on the hills and mountains, it has dominated the way of life and the eating habits in this area for centuries.

The delicately balanced economic unit of the croft, as it was prior to the point when the Highlands were 'cleared' of people in the 19th century, was based on self-sufficiency. A crofting family of the 18th century reared cattle, sheep, poultry, goats and hens. During the winter months the animals were kept alive on whatever was available round the croft, but in the summer the family would take them all up into the mountains to a hut called the *sheiling* where they lived for a few months while the animals enjoyed the sweet summer pastures and the clear mountain air. This meant that the valuable and scarce patches of arable land could be used for growing crops such as potatoes, turnips, oats or barley.

The cattle, goats, and sheep meanwhile produced milk which was made into cheese and butter, and the sheep produced valuable wool for spinning and weaving. Cattle were a necessary source of outside income, often exchanged for corn (oatmeal), and driven to markets in the South along the ancient drove roads through gaps in the mountains like the Bealach-na-Ba ('The Pass of the Cattle') in Wester Ross.

STOCK-BREEDING

These Scottish mountain cattle were the domesticated descendants of the ancient breed of the forests. They were originally black and much smaller, shaggier and hardier than today's Highland cattle. Similarly, the sheep kept by the poor crofter was quite a different animal to the one that is to be found all over the Highlands today. The breed which was indigenous to the Highlands was known as the Chaoirich Bhega ('Little Sheep'). They had pink noses, and very fine wool, but they were very small, weighing only about

30 lb (13.5 kg). They were a variety of colours: pure white, black, grey or brown and sometimes a mixture. The main point in their favour was their tameness, which meant that they could therefore be milked easily. The mutton from these sheep was highly prized for its flavour.

Goats were kept in much greater numbers than sheep, since they provided a large proportion of the household milk supply. They also suited the environment, being nimble and sure-footed in the mountains. At the end of the 17th century 100,000 goat and kid skins were sent to London in one year from the Highlands.

Everyone kept hens, which scratched a living from the leftovers and provided a valuable supply of eggs. They were also very convenient for the pot and one was often quickly killed, cleaned and plucked when unexpected visitors arrived.

In this type of self-sufficiency one would expect to find pigs, but in the Highlands there was a universal prejudice against pigmeat. The reason is hard to find, but there are several theories, including the Biblical prohibitions against it. Among superstitious people the pig was regarded as a bad omen and this probably was the main influence against it. Nor were the climate and terrain very suitable for it.

DIET AND COOKERY

Few Highland crofts of the period had chimneys. The fire usually burnt on a central hearth and the smoke escaped, if at all, through chinks in the rafters. The main fuel was peat, cut and dried till hard. It provided a gentle, constant heat which was perfect for simmering the pot of broth or porridge which hung by a chain from the roof over the heat. The other piece of cooking equipment was a girdle, also suspended from the ceiling, and on this they baked the thin, crisp oatcakes and thicker bannocks which were so much part of the staple diet.

Fish, shellfish and seaweed supplemented the diet throughout the year. Game was enjoyed by the laird, but the crofter saw little of it unless it was poached. Today, eating traditions in the Highlands have changed dramatically from almost total self-sufficiency to dependence on outside supplies of food. In spite of this the indigenous Celtic people of the Highlands still have a tendency to boil and stew rather than roast and grill. The women are still as skilful in their use of the girdle. Families still make use of the rich harvest of the sea to supplement

THE HIGHLANDS AND INNER HEBRIDES

their diet and, even if the children today do not actually satisfy their hunger with Red Dulse, their grandparents can remember the distinctive flavour of the raw sea-weed picked fresh from the shore.

FISH

Herring and Mackerel

Though supplies of herring have gradually diminished over the years the West Coast herring is still regarded as the finest and has always been an important item of the Highland diet.

Herring and mackerel are fish which lose their bloom quickly. The firm, bright skin soon becomes dull and flabby and the rich flavour of the fresh fish is lost. Easily the best herring and mackerel are the ones which you catch yourself or collect from the pier as the fishing boats unload.

The quality of the fish depends also on the time of year, since it is important to enjoy them when the fat content is high – as much as twenty per cent after the fish has been feeding for a month or two, rather than after spawning when it can be as low as two per cent. They spawn either in the spring or autumn so that the spring-spawning fish are at their best from July through to February while the autumn-spawning fish are best eaten from April through the summer to September or October. The West Coast herring are autumn-spawning fish, whilst mackerel caught in British waters spawn in the spring, so they are at their best through the winter months.

Fried West Coast Herring (or Mackerel)

8 medium or 4 large   Salt and pepper
   herring (or mackerel)   Fat or oil for frying
Fine or medium oatmeal
   for coating

Wash, gut and bone the fish if they are whole. Put some oatmeal onto a plate and season well. Press the fish into the oatmeal on both sides. Melt a little fat in the frying pan and when hot place the fish in, flesh side down. Cook quickly for 3–5 minutes depending on the thickness of the fish. Turn and cook on the other side for the same time. Serve with oatcakes.

The traditional Highland way to eat these fish, as in other parts of the country, is coated in oatmeal and fried. They should be golden brown and crisp on the outside, soft and juicy inside. If the fat content is very high, they almost fry in their own fat.

Kippers

At the major fishing ports on the coast, such as Ullapool,

Mallaig, Oban and Tarbert, smoke-houses transform the humble herring into the famous West Coast Kipper, often known as a Loch Fyne Kipper since this is where the finest are to be found. They are made from fat herring with the guts and gills removed, split open down the back from head to tail, lightly brined, often dyed and cold-smoked for about four hours. Some undyed, oak-smoked kippers are made but most of them are dyed to give a rich mahogany colour which the market demands. This colour could not be achieved by smoking without losing a lot of weight and producing a drier, stronger-flavoured product which is presumably more like the original cure. They are usually grilled plainly or fried in butter and are often just 'a meal in themselves'.

Salt Herring

Kippers are a relatively modern invention compared with the salt-pickled herring which was the important cure in the area and a staple item of the crofter's diet in winter months. When the shoals of herring came into the loch, nets were put out and it was a communal job to bring in the fish and share it among the village. Excess supplies were salted in wooden barrels by the women (see p. 68). so every croft had its own barrel in some corner of a shed.

The salt herring was mostly boiled with potatoes but it was also eaten raw as in Scandinavian countries. Usually it was eaten straight from the barrel. Today this is not so common, though there is no reason why we should not use salt herring instead of salted anchovies when the occasion arises. People in the Highland area are still fond of salt herring and many of them salt their own when the herring come into the loch, often using large plastic bins rather than wooden barrels which are difficult to find today.

Salt-pickled Herring

Mackerel, cod or conger eel are also salted in this way.

Herring, with only the gut removed	A large wooden barrel or plastic bucket
Coarse salt	or bin

Shovel in a layer of salt then place on a layer of fish. Lay them with their backs uppermost but slightly on their sides. Put in the next layer of salt then the fish lying in the opposite direction. Continue in layers till the barrel is full. Cover and remove fish as you need it.

To cook the fish, wash and soak them in cold water overnight. Put them into a pan, cover with water and bring gently to simmering point. Simmer for about 10 minutes. Drain and eat with boiled jacket potatoes.

In some parts of the country the herring are cooked in a pot with the potatoes. The herring are placed on top of the potatoes or they might be put in layers with them so that they flavour the potatoes. Most West coast housewives now seem to prefer cooking them separately.

Smoked Mackerel

An increasing amount of mackerel is being smoked, as the demand for this alternative to the herring increases. They may be either hot-smoked or kippered. The hot-smoked variety are headed, gutted and left whole then brined and smoked for three to three-and-a-half hours, depending on the size of the fish, till it is cooked through and a golden brown colour. Kippered mackerel are split down the back in the same way as herring, or block fillets are cut from the fish. They are then brined and cold-smoked for two-and-a-half hours if they are fillets, four hours if they are split fish.

Potted Smoked Mackerel

12 oz skinned and boned hot-smoked mackerel (350 g)	1 clove of garlic
	Lemon juice to taste
	Salt and pepper
5 oz unsalted butter (150 g)	Clarified butter for covering

The flavour of the mackerel combines well with lemon and garlic in this fish paste, which can be used as a high tea dish with a salad or as an appetiser with hot toast and butter.

Soften the butter and place in a liquidiser with the mackerel and garlic. Blend together for a smooth consistency. Season with salt, pepper and lemon juice. Place in small individual pots and cover with a thin layer of clarified butter. Serve with hot toast or a salad.

Shellfish

Mussels, razor fish, clabby dhus (horse mussels), whelks and cockles are boiled and eaten with vinegar, salt and pepper. After they have been boiled and removed from the cooking liquid it is allowed to settle and the clear liquid poured off and taken as a drink. Sometimes a soup is made with shellfish using rice and the same method as Partan Bree (see p. 31).

In some Highland minds shellfish are inextricably

linked with poverty and the last stages of hunger, when there was nothing left on the land. Despite memories of widespread poverty many have overcome their prejudices and they are often eaten today. Prawns (Dublin Bay Prawns or Norwegian Lobsters, as they are also called) and lobsters are an important source of income to the area. They are practically all exported to markets on the mainland and abroad as the quality and flavour is so fine.

This coastline is also an ideal place for oysters and there were at one time some natural oyster beds here. Today the Pacific oyster is being farmed commercially with some success, but not in large enough quantities yet to satisfy the Scottish demand.

Islay Scallops

16 scallops	4 oz butter (125 g)
3 tbsp milk	1 tbsp lemon juice
2 oz seasoned flour (50 g)	

Garnish –
Chopped parsley

Scallops are exported, particularly from Islay, but they are not quite so expensive as oysters and local people enjoy them simply cooked in butter. They are available from October to March and are at their best in January and February. Usually they are sold opened and have a firm, creamy-white flesh with a bright orange roe.

If the white muscle is very thick, slice into two across the grain to make two thinner rounds. Now dip this and the pink coral part in milk and then toss in seasoned flour.

Heat half of the butter in a frying pan and fry the scallops very gently for 2–3 minutes on each side. Place in a heated serving dish.

Add the remaining butter and heat until it just begins to turn a nut-brown colour. Add lemon juice and pour over the scallops. Garnish with parsley and serve.

Limpet Stovies

4 pt limpets (2½ L)	Salt and pepper
Peeled potatoes	2 oz butter (50 g)

Yet another regional version of Stovies. Limpets are found clinging to rocks and can be prised off with a knife or a stone. They are quite tough, so this is a good way of cooking them.

Soak limpets overnight in fresh, cold water. Drain and put in a pan. Cover with water, add salt and bring to the boil. Simmer till they come out of their shells. Rinse in cold water, remove eyes and sandy trails.

Weigh the limpets and take three times the amount of peeled potatoes. Put a layer of sliced potatoes in a pan. Add a layer of limpets and season with salt and pepper. Continue in layers, finishing with a layer of potatoes. Add two cups of the cooking liquor. Top with pieces of butter. Cover with a tightly-fitting lid and simmer for 1 hour. Garnish with parsley and serve.

Crappit Head or Croppen Head

4 large fish heads
Fish liver
Oatmeal

Onion or spring onion,
  finely chopped
Salt and pepper

When very large cod or haddock or other similar white fish were caught it was not in the Highlander's nature to throw anything away. Hence this method of using the very valuable liver from the white fish. The liver melts away into the oatmeal when it is cooked and the bones from the head also add flavour to a dish which is not only highly nutritious but also has a unique flavour. The old Scots word Crap *meant to 'fill' or 'stuff'.*

Place the fish liver in a bowl and cover with cold water. Add some salt and soak for 1 hour. Strain. Add oatmeal and onion to the fish liver to make a fairly thick consistency. Season to taste.

Place the mixture in a cleaned head and tie up with string. Begin by tying a sort of noose round its mouth to keep the jaws together then take the string over the top of the head and tie another noose round the centre of the head. Finally tie up the remains of the stomach bag, which will be at the back of the head. Wrap in foil and put in a pan of boiling water and simmer for 30 minutes.

Serve the head on its own or with portions of plain boiled fish. Sometimes the stuffing is boiled as for a cloutie dumpling in a cloth and eaten with the boiled fish.

Highland Fish Sauce

15 anchovies
½ pt wine vinegar
  (250 ml)
1 pt red wine (500 ml)
1 tbsp horseradish,
  scraped
2 small onions, chopped
2 tbsp parsley, finely
  chopped

1 dsp lemon thyme
2 bay leaves
1 grated nutmeg
½ tsp ground mace
9 cloves
1 tsp freshly ground
  black pepper

This is a store sauce from a 19th-century Laird's kitchen.

Chop up anchovies and add to the vinegar. Cover and leave for a week, shaking occasionally.

Put this into a pan and add all the other ingredients. Simmer for about ½ hr.

Strain through a fine sieve. Add a little cochineal to improve the colour if necessary. Cool and store in a bottle.

To use, shake the bottle well, melt 2 oz butter (50 g) in a pan and add 1 tbsp of the sauce. Serve hot with fish.

The salmon season lasts from February through the summer to September, with variations for rod-caught fish on some rivers. It is at its best from May to July and this is the time to grill salmon. The fish has plenty of fat and the flavour is good. Steaks from the middle or tail are best. Both salmon and sea trout are exported in large quantities to affluent markets around the world. The Highlanders themselves see little of them.

Grilled Salmon Steaks

4×6 oz ¾" salmon steaks   Salt and pepper
  (175 g 2 cm)
2 oz melted butter
  (50 g)

Garnish –
Parsley sprigs, lemon slices and pats of butter

Wipe the fish with a damp cloth and then brush on one side with melted butter, season with salt and pepper and put under a hot grill. Grill for about 4 minutes then turn. Brush second side with melted butter, season and grill for about another 4 minutes.

Serve on a hot ashet garnished with pats of butter, parsley and lemon.

GAME

Grouse moor and deer forest cover the greatest area of the Central Highlands. The region may not have many agricultural resources but it does produce the finest game to be found anywhere in the world. Shooting and fishing estates are huge, covering thousands of acres. Cooking and eating game is reserved mainly for the few who enjoy the sport and also for those who can afford it when it reaches the market or hotel dining room.

Venison

This word describes several varieties of deer which have their own season in Scotland. The most common deer in the Highlands is the red deer, now being farmed commercially in the Grampians. The stag season lasts from the 1st July to 20th October and the animal is at its best in early autumn after a summer of good feeding, but just before the rutting season when its flavour becomes very strong. For roasting, the meat should be from a young stag one-and-a-half to two years old. The lean meat should be dark red, close-grained with firm white fat. It is usually sold in joints. Leg and saddle are the choice cuts for roasting; loin chops, neck and shoulder joints can be braised or stewed. The meat should hang for two to three weeks before use and, provided this is done (and the meat is from a young animal), it should roast well. Old animals shot early in the season with very little fat can be dry and tough if roasted, so it is important to check with the butcher or gamekeeper on the history of the meat.

The red deer hind season lasts from the 21st October

to the 15th February. There is less fat and less flavour to the hind meat compared with stag, and the joints are smaller. Other deer include the roe deer, where the buck season lasts from 1st May to 20th October and the doe from 21st October to 28–29th February. The fallow deer buck season is from 1st August to 30th April and the doe from 21st October to 15th February.

Sutherland Venison

3–4 lb haunch of red deer venison, boned (1½–2 kg)
Salt and pepper
2 oz butter (50 g)
For the suet paste covering –
2 lb self-raising flour (1 kg)

1 lb suet, finely chopped (500 g)
Salt and freshly ground black pepper
Cold water to mix

Preheat the oven to 350°F/180°C or gas mark 4

Season the haunch and melt the butter in a large roasting tin. You will need a grid in the tin to keep the venison off the bottom.

To make up the pastry, sift the flour into a bowl and add salt and pepper. Add suet and mix through. Now add enough water to make a firm dough. If it is too soft it will be difficult to handle. Turn out onto a floured board. Dust the top with flour and roll out into a large circle about ½" (1 cm) thick. Lay the joint in the centre and wrap the pastry round the meat, sealing with water where necessary. Place this on the grid with the joins underneath. Put in a moderate oven and allow 20 minutes per lb. Baste the top with melted butter from time to time. To serve, remove from the oven and leave in a warm place for at least 15 minutes to let the juices settle. Cut off the paste and carve the venison. Serve pieces of the paste with the meat and crab apple or rowan berry jelly. Season the remaining pan juices and pour into a heated sauce boat. Serve with the meat.

Rowan Jelly

2 lb almost-ripe rowan berries (1 kg)
2 lb unpeeled cooking apples (1 kg)

1 lb (450 g) preserving sugar to 1 pt (½ L) juice

The rowans are best picked in the autumn, just before they change colour from orange to dark red, when they become much more bitter.

Remove any excess stalk from the rowans and chop the

apples roughly. Put into a preserving pan and just cover with water.

Simmer until the fruit is tender. Strain through a scalded jelly bag or muslin. Leave until the dripping has stopped. Do not squeeze the bag or the jelly will be cloudy. Measure the juice, return to the pan and add sugar. Stir over a low heat till the sugar has dissolved. Boil rapidly, stirring occasionally and skimming when necessary.

To test for setting, place a little on a saucer and allow to cool. Very gently push your finger through the jelly and the surface should wrinkle when it is ready to set. Pour into heated jars. Cover and store.

Venison Roll

Often the less choice cuts or the innards found their way onto the crofter's tables, when a kind of pudding rather like a venison haggis would have been boiled in a cloth. This recipe uses a baking method which is equally successful. Venison liver has a rich flavour and is regarded as a great delicacy.

1 lb venison, flank or shoulder (500 g)	2–3 tomatoes
1 lb venison heart (500 g)	Grated rind of 1 lemon
1 lb venison liver (500 g)	2 oz fresh breadcrumbs (50 g)
2–3 medium onions	2 eggs
1 lb streaky bacon, finely diced (500 g)	Salt and pepper
	Some browned crumbs
	2 oz dripping (50 g)

Preheat the oven to 375°F/190°C or gas mark 5

Mince shoulder or flank, heart, liver and onions together. Skin and dice tomatoes. Put minced meats, onion, bacon, tomatoes, lemon rind, breadcrumbs, eggs and seasoning into a large bowl and mix thoroughly.

Shape into a roll and cover with browned crumbs. Melt the dripping in a roasting tin and put in roll. Baste roll with some dripping, cover with foil and bake in a hot oven for 1½–2 hours. Serves 12–14, hot or cold.

Pocha Buidhe

Even the least energetic members of a shooting party will rush to a burn to clean out the stomach bag after a deer has been gralloched (removing the innards from the carcass). Deer tripe is finely grained, with a quite distinctive flavour, very different and much superior to cow's tripe. The Gaelic name means 'yellow bag'.

1 deer tripe	Salt and pepper
2 pt milk (1 L)	Triangles of buttered toast
4 oz butter (100 g)	Finely chopped parsley
4 oz flour (100 g)	
1 lb onions, finely chopped (500 g)	

To prepare the tripe the stomach bag must be removed from the animal and cleaned out under running water *immediately*, hence the need for a burn nearby. Soak in cold water for 24 hours before using.

Boil the tripe very gently for 6–8 hours in plenty of boiling water. Remove and cut into 1"–1½" (2.5–4 cm) squares. Cook the onions in butter in a large pan without browning them. Add the flour and remove from the heat. Gradually stir in the milk. Add the tripe and seasoning and simmer gently for 1–1½ hours. Serve on triangles of hot, buttered toast and garnish with finely chopped parsley.

Red Grouse

With its rich, gamey flavour of heather and moorland this is the most sought-after game bird and is regarded as something of an aristocrat among other birds. The first day's grouse shooting heralds the beginning of the season and it is celebrated in the evening when the first grouse shot appear on the dining table. They are regarded as such delicacies that they are flown by plane to distant kitchens so that the ritual of the 'glorious 12th' may be observed.

This, of course, means the 12th of August when the season starts. It ends on the 10th December and the birds are at their best from August to October. Each bird weighs between 1¼–1½ lb (600–750 g) which usually makes one serving. They should be hung for 2–4 days, depending on the weather. If it is hot and humid, reduce the hanging time. To judge the age of the bird look at the two outer primary feathers, which will be rounded and tattered if old, pointed if young.

Roast Red Grouse

2 brace of young grouse   Berries (brambles,
4 oz butter (125 g)   raspberries,
Salt and pepper   rowanberries,
8 slices of fat bacon   cranberries)
4 slices of buttered
   bread

Preheat the oven to 375°F/190°C or gas mark 5

Mix the butter with the berries and put about a quarter into the body cavity of each bird. Lay strips of bacon on the breast and place each bird on a slice of buttered bread in a roasting tin. Put in a moderately hot oven and roast for 35–40 minutes depending on the size of the grouse. Remove the bacon 10 minutes before the bird is ready, to brown the breast. Baste frequently throughout the roasting.

Serve with the gravy, bread sauce, fried bread-crumbs, crisps and a green salad. Rowan and apple jelly is also very good with grouse. A croûton of bread fried in butter with the cooked mashed liver spread on it is sometimes used as a base for the bird to sit on when served.

Grampian Grouse Pudding

An ideal way of using old birds, the long, slow cooking develops the flavours as well as tenderising the meat.

2 old grouse	1–2 tbsp madeira or port
1 lb rump steak (500 g)	Salt and pepper
1 oz seasoned flour	*For the pastry –*
(25 g)	12 oz self-raising
1 bay leaf	flour (350 g)
Some peppercorns	6 oz suet, finely
1 medium onion,	chopped (175 g)
finely chopped	Salt and pepper
2 oz mushrooms, stalks	Water to mix
removed (50 g)	

Begin by stripping the meat from the grouse. Chop this and the beef into small pieces and toss in seasoned flour. Put the grouse carcass and bones into the pan, add a bay leaf and some peppercorns. Just cover with water and simmer for an hour to make some stock. Leave to cool.

When you are ready to make up the pie, start with the pastry. Sift the flour into a bowl and add the suet, salt and pepper. Make sure that the water is cold and add enough to make a soft, elastic dough. Turn out onto a floured board, dust the top with flour and knead lightly. Cut off $^1/_3$ for the lid then roll out the remainder to fit into a greased $2\frac{1}{2}$ pt pudding bowl ($1\frac{1}{4}$ L).

Next fill up the bowl with the grouse, beef, onion, mushrooms, salt and pepper. Fill up with madeira or port and stock. Cover with remaining pastry and seal edges with some water. Make a hole in the centre and cover with a piece of foil which has a pleat in the middle to allow for expansion. Tie with string and steam for 4–6 hours until the grouse is tender. After 2–3 hours remove the foil and fill up with more stock through the hole in the lid. Serve on a heated ashet with a white napkin round the bowl.

Pheasant

Not a bird of the high moors, the pheasant keeps to lower land and feeds on less exotic fare compared with the grouse. Its flavour is not so strong and the carcass is much larger. The cock bird might be 3–3¼ lb (1.5–1.6 kg), which could serve 3–4 people. The hen bird is smaller, about 2–2½ lb (1–1.5 kg) and is regarded as better flavoured than the cock. The pheasant season lasts from 1st October to 1st February and the birds are in prime condition about November and December. They should be hung for 10–14 days, depending on the age of the bird; you can tell a young bird by its pliable beak and feet.

Roast Pheasant

2 young pheasant
4 rashers of streaky
    bacon
1 oz butter (25 g)
Salt and pepper
For stuffing the cavity –
4 oz butter, softened
    (125 g)

Juice of 1 lemon
Salt and freshly milled
    black pepper
For the gravy –
½ pt water or game stock
    (250 ml)
2–3 tbsp port or red wine
Salt and pepper

Garnish –
Game chips and watercress

Preheat the oven to 375°F/190°C or gas mark 5

To make the stuffing, mix the butter and lemon juice together and season well with salt and pepper. Put half of this into each bird. Truss each carcass.

Place butter in roasting tin and heat. Season birds and roll in butter. Place leg side down and roast in a hot oven for 15–20 minutes. Turn over onto the other leg for another 15–20 minutes, basting frequently. Turn the birds onto their backs, cover the breasts with bacon and roast for a final 15–20 minutes. Remove the bacon for a few minutes at the end to brown the breasts.

Place the birds in a heated serving ashet and leave for 10 minutes in a warm place before carving.

Meanwhile make up the gravy. Pour off the surplus fat from the roasting tin then add water or game stock and boil up, scraping the pan to incorporate all the sediment. Add a little port or some red wine, if available, and boil for a few minutes. Check seasoning and strain into a heated sauceboat. Serve with breadcrumbs tossed in butter, and/or bread sauce and gravy.

Highland Game Soup

A clear soup with a rich flavour.

4 lb well-hung game bones (2 kg)	Some parsley stalks
1 lb shin of beef, minced (500 g)	4 oz celery, chopped (125 g)
Giblets of game birds, if available	4 oz white of leek, chopped (125 g)
2–3 carrots, sliced	1 doz peppercorns
2 medium onions, sliced	Salt
2 bay leaves	Cold water
	Port wine to taste

Garnish –
Diced cooked game meat

Brown the bones and onions in the oven or in a frying pan on top of the stove. Place in a large pot with the beef, giblets, carrots, celery, leeks, bay leaves, parsley, peppercorns and salt. Cover with cold water. Bring to the boil and simmer for about 4–5 hours, skimming when necessary. Do not stir. Leave to cool a little and settle, then strain through a fine muslin. Skim well, removing all the grease, then add the port and check seasoning. Garnish with diced cooked game meat. Serves 12–14.

Other Scottish Game Birds and their seasons

Blackgame, Blackcock or Black Grouse: August 20th to December 10th – up to 4 lb (2 kg).

Capercailzie or Wood Grouse: October 1st to January 31st – up to 4 lb (2 kg).

Partridge: September 1st to February 1st – approx. weight ½–1 lb (125–250 g).

Wood Pigeon: no close season.

Ptarmigan or White Grouse: August 12th to December 10th – approx. weight 8–12 oz (250–350 g).

Common Snipe: August 12th to January 31st – approx. weight 2–10 oz (50–300 g).

Mallard, Teal and Widgeon Ducks: up to 3 lb (1½ kg); *Pinkfooted and Greylag Geese:* Below high-tide mark the season for ducks and geese is from September 1st to February 20th and elsewhere from September 1st to January 31st.

MEAT, VEGETABLES AND POULTRY

Meat was an occasional luxury to the Highland crofter, as he may only have tasted it in its fresh state once a year when an animal was killed and salted down for the winter. This was usually mutton rather than beef and often the leg was dry-salted to make a Mutton Ham.

The fresh or salted meat would have been boiled in the pot to make a broth with whatever vegetables or grains were available. The range of vegetables was limited. Potatoes were more or less universal by about 1785, but they never dominated the diet to the same extent as in Ireland where they became almost the only food of the peasants. The safe, hardy vegetables like carrots and turnips were grown latterly with some leeks and onions, but the original green vegetable of the Highlander was nettles. He grew his own patch of them which were used in the spring, when they were very young and tender and were thought to purify the blood and ensure good health throughout the year.

Nettle Kail

2½–3 lb boiling fowl (1¼–1½ kg)
1 lb young nettles or spinach (500 g)
4 pts water (2¼ L)
1 oz barley meal or fine oatmeal (25 g)
Salt and pepper
For the stuffing –
6 oz medium oatmeal (175 g)

2 oz fat (suet, dripping or butter) (50 g)
1 medium onion, finely chopped
Salt and pepper
1 tbsp wild garlic leaves or mint leaves, chopped

This was made with a year-old cockerel, and in some areas families gathered for Nettle Kail suppers on Shrove Tuesday to bless the spring work. In this recipe spinach can be substituted for nettles, but when available they make an interesting soup.

Kail is a word used loosely for greens of any kind, or for the soup made with them, and does not therefore always refer to the vegetable-kale.

To make up the stuffing, melt the fat in a pan and fry the onions till cooked but not brown. Add the oatmeal and cook for a few minutes. Season and add garlic or mint.

Stuff the body cavity of the bird and skewer or tie up opening. Put the bird into a large pot and add water, salt and pepper. Bring to the boil and simmer for 1–1½ hours.

To prepare the nettles or spinach, wash very well, dry and chop up finely. When the chicken is almost cooked, put in the barley flour or oatmeal and nettles or spinach. Simmer for about 10 minutes.

To serve the chicken, remove from the pot and place on a heated ashet. Remove about half the nettles with a slotted spoon and place in another dish. Add a knob of butter and a little of the cooking liquor. Serve with the chicken.

The remaining broth can be served as it is the next day or it can be puréed in the liquidiser or passed through a sieve. Some finely chopped chicken meat can be added for garnish.

Chicken Stovies

Sometimes known as Stoved Chicken, this Highland dish combines potatoes with chicken using a typical cooking method. The name comes from the early use of the word as a method of cooking, referring to anything which was put on the stove. '... add the boiling water and let the preparation stove slowly till wanted.' (Meg Dods)

4 chicken joints
2 tbsp seasoned flour
2 oz butter (50 g)
1 lb onions, sliced (500 g)

2 lb potatoes, peeled and sliced (1 kg)
½ pt chicken stock or water (250 ml)

Garnish –
Chopped parsley

Preheat the oven to 350°F/180°C or gas mark 4

Flour the chicken and brown lightly in the butter in a frying pan. Place a layer of potatoes and onions in a casserole, season and place two joints on top. Cover with a layer of potatoes and onions, season and add two other joints. Pour over remaining butter in frying pan and finish with a layer of potatoes. Add stock or water. Cover with a tight-fitting lid and bake for 1½ hours in a moderate oven.

Remove lid towards the end of the cooking time, brush potatoes with a little melted butter and allow to brown on top by leaving off the lid. Sprinkle with parsley and serve.

Highland Beef Balls

The original recipe uses saltpetre and coats the balls in melted suet so that they were expected to keep. The addition of a finely chopped onion improves the flavour and texture. In Shetland they make a very similar spiced meat called Brönies.

1 lb mince (500 g)
2 oz suet, finely chopped (50 g)
1 tsp freshly ground black pepper

1 tsp mixed spice
1 tsp salt
½ tsp sugar
½ tsp ginger
¼ tsp ground cloves

Mix all the ingredients thoroughly together in a mixing bowl. Shape into 4 large or 8 small patties. Fry for five minutes on both sides in a little hot fat. Serve with bacon and Skirlie (see p. 77).

Highland Colcannon

*'Did ye ever ate colcannon thats made from thickened cream,
With greens and scallions blended like a picture in your dream?'*

(Irish rhyme)

1 lb kale or cabbage (500 g)
1 lb potatoes (500 g)
2 small leeks, finely chopped

¼ pt single cream (125 ml)
2 oz butter (50 g)
Salt and pepper

Cook the kale or cabbage and potatoes separately. Meanwhile simmer the leeks gently in the cream until they are just soft. Drain and mash the potatoes and add the leeks and cream. Drain the kale or cabbage and blend into the potatoes, beating over a low heat till it is light and fluffy. Season and pile into a heated serving dish. Make a well in the centre and pour in some melted butter. Serve with spoonfuls of the butter. Fry leftovers in bacon fat till crisp and brown.

This dish illustrates the Celtic links with Ireland since it is the same as the Irish eat at Hallowe'en with charms in it. Scallions are leeks.

Pan White Pudding

3–4 oz roast dripping (75–100 g)	Salt and pepper
1 large onion, cut in thin slices	6–8 oz medium oatmeal (175–250 g)

Melt dripping in frying pan and when hot add onion. Fry gently till the onion is cooked but not browned. Add oatmeal and seasonings, stir well. Cook for a few minutes, stirring occasionally. May be served with roast meats or game or with stews.

This version of Skirlie from Mull was traditionally eaten with boiled potatoes for dinner, in the middle of the day, or for tea at night on toast. It differs from the North-Eastern version (see p. 77) in its use of dripping rather than suet.

DAIRY PRODUCE

Milk, whey and buttermilk were drunk in great quantities, and 18th-century travellers in the Highlands noticed the extensive use of milk and milk products compared with Southern Scotland and England.

The traditional cheeses of the Highlands are soft ones. Only in the southern islands of the Inner Hebrides, which are in more contact with Lowland Scotland and in particular the dairying areas of Ayrshire, are hard-pressed cheeses found. On Gigha, Islay and Arran and also in Campbeltown, there are creameries producing the Cheddar-type cheese and the less mature, moister Dunlop.

The little island of Gigha has nine farms which provide the local creamery with raw, unpasteurised milk to make the cheese. The creamery began producing cheese in 1942 and today it is made mostly in 40 lb blocks which are sent to the Glasgow cheese-market to be graded. They also produce some 5 lb round, cloth-bound traditional cheeses known as *truckles*, which they sell in their local shop.

The Islay creamery produces small, round, one-pound cheeses known as *Islay Dunlop* in addition to the large blocks of cheddar. At the Torrylinn creamery on Arran they also make the large cheddar blocks. Pressure from the local community encouraged them to produce a smaller, more distinctively local cheese and they now sell about fifty thousand, 2¼ lb (1 kg) *Arran Dunlops* a year. In character they are somewhere between the mature Cheddar and the milder, less mature Dunlop.

CROWDIE

Eighteenth-century Scots mixed meal and water together and made Crowdie. This gruel or brose was the staple item of diet for most of the population. Therefore the name was transferred from the dish to food in general and people talked about *Crowdie-time* as a time to eat. Because it took on this much broader meaning it seems that all kinds of dishes had the word Crowdie added to them. *Crowdie-Mowdie* was a kind of steamed porridge made with milk. *Cream-Crowdie* or Crannachan was a special dish of harvest plenty when cream and oatmeal were mixed. *Ale Crowdie* was a mixture of ale, oatmeal, treacle and whisky, also a harvest dish.

While these terms were national ones in some parts of the Highlands a dish called *Crowdie-Butter* was made. Dr John Jamieson, referring to it in the *Dictionary of the Scottish Language* in 1818 says that 'In Ross-shire it denotes curds with the whey pressed out, mixed with butter nearly in an equal proportion.' Crowdie as a cheese, therefore, has had a very long association with the Highlands. Leave out the butter and it is the same as the soft, fresh cheese which we immediately associate with the name today.

In the Highlands it was a crofter's cheese made with surplus fresh milk which was allowed to sour naturally in a warm place. It was then heated very gently till it 'scrambled' or separated. The curd and whey was put into a large muslin bag and hung from the branch of a tree, preferably a rowan. When all the whey had dripped out then it was ready to eat. Besides butter, wild herbs and berries were often mixed through and also cream. Usually it was pressed into a mould then turned out, and cut in slices and eaten with oatcakes and bannocks.

At Tain, in Ross-shire, the selection of Highland Fine Cheeses which are made commercially by the creamery have preserved the original traditions of Crowdie making. Rennet is not used, as in other cheeses, to speed up the souring process, and because of this natural curding the cheese has a lovely citric flavour.

The *Highland Crowdie* is a low-fat cheese. When skimmed on the croft a little cream was always left so it was not strictly a skimmed milk cheese. *Crowdie and Cream* is a mixture of two parts crowdie to one part fresh double cream. *Crowdie and Wild Garlic* has the chopped wild garlic leaf added. Of the richer varieties *Highland Soft* is a mild-flavoured, full-fat soft cheese used for cheesecake and sweets. *Hramsa,* the Gaelic word for 'wild garlic', the ancient all-healing herb, is a full-fat soft cheese with cream and chopped garlic leaves added. *Galic* is similar except that it is a cylinder shape and rolled in flaked oats, crumbled almonds and hazel nuts. *Caboc* is a rich, double-cream cheese, rolled in toasted pin-head oatmeal, and it was the chieftan's cheese. The recipe from which it is made has been handed down through many generations and is now one of Highland Fine Cheeses' most famous products.

Tatties and Crowdie

2 lb floury potatoes peeled (1 kg)	1 tbsp spring onions or chives, finely chopped	*A main meal dish.*
1 oz butter (25 g)	1 tbsp double cream	
4 oz crowdie (125 g)	Salt and pepper	

Garnish –
Chopped parsley

Put potatoes into a pan, add salt and boil in the usual way. Drain and dry off. Put into a large soup tureen. Dot pieces of butter on top and sprinkle with finely-chopped parsley. Cover with lid and serve hot.

Add double cream to the crowdie, season and add spring onions or chives. Serve this in a separate bowl with the potatoes. Any leftovers can be mixed together and served cold as a potato salad.

Hatted or Added Kit

2 pts buttermilk (1 L)	Grated nutmeg to taste	*This very old Highland dish was*
1 pt milk (500 ml)	$\frac{1}{4}$–$\frac{1}{2}$ pt double cream	*made by milking the cow onto*
3 dsp rennet	(125–250 ml)	*a bowl of warm buttermilk. The*
2 oz sugar (50 g)		*following recipe works quite*

Put the buttermilk and milk into a large pan and heat very gently till it is just blood heat. Remove from the heat and add rennet. Pour into a bowl and leave over-night. By the next day the curd will have formed and separated from the whey. Pour through a fine nylon or

well without a cow, but Highlanders consider that direct milking puts a better 'hat' on the kit. The basis of the dish is a soft-curd cheese which can be served with fruit as a sweet dish.

Sometimes it was flavoured with malt whisky and eaten with oatcakes.

hair sieve and allow the whey to drain off. Leave for at least 24 hours. The curd should now be fairly stiff. Season this with some sugar and nutmeg.

Whip up cream till stiff and add sugar and nutmeg to taste. Mix the two very gently together. Chill and serve with any kind of fresh or stewed fruit. It is very good with a fruit salad.

The above quantities make about 12 oz (350 g) of curd which need not be used all at once since it keeps very well in a cold place for about a fortnight.

SOME DEVELOPMENTS OF THE ORIGINAL CROWDIE

From the meal-and-water Crowdie many local variations have developed which are just extensions of the original concept. The common element throughout them all is oatmeal and the fact that they are all mixed together in a bowl – a quick and easy way of preparing food when cooking facilities are limited.

In the following recipes fruit, cream, soft cheeses, whisky and honey are combined in a variety of ways. There are no hard and fast rules about quantities; it is very much a question of testing and trying till you find your favourite mixture.

This recipe comes from Trotternish in Skye. It was such a speciality of the area that the MacLeods gave Trotternish the Gaelic name Duthaich nan Stapag, ('Land of the Crowdie'). It was a special treat, eaten in times of plenty like harvest time or at a celebration.

Stapag Uachair (Crowdie Cream)

1 pt fresh cream (250 ml)	Caster Sugar
Medium oatmeal, toasted	Talisker whisky

Beat up the cream till stiff. Usually each person was given a bowl of cream and the oatmeal, whisky and sugar was added according to taste.

This was sometimes used as a kind of cheese spread on oatcakes or it was eaten with some kind of sharp fruit like rhubarb, gooseberries or raspberries.

Fuarag

½ pt soured cream (250 ml)	Sugar to taste
2 oz medium oatmeal (50 g)	

Toast the oatmeal lightly under a grill or in the oven. Leave to cool

Add to the cream, add sugar to taste and leave for several hours till it thickens.

Cream-Crowdie or Crannachan

2 oz medium oatmeal (50 g)
2½ fl oz malt whisky (75 ml)
2 tbsp thick heather honey
2 oz cream cheese or crowdie (50 g)

4 oz fresh raspberries (125 g) or other soft fruit
¼ pt double cream (150 ml)
4 tsp clear heather honey

Steep the oatmeal in malt whisky and thick honey overnight. Mix in the raspberries and cream cheese. Beat the cream till stiff and put a spoonful in the base of a wine goblet. Put the oatmeal and honey mixture on top and finish with the remaining cream. Make a slight well in the centre and pour in the clear honey. Serve.

There are many varieties of this now, though it was at one time made at Harvest-time or Hallowe'en when charms were mixed through it. Eager children would consume it in vast quantities in the hope of finding a lucky charm. This recipe is certainly not suitable for children, but the combination of flavours make it a delicious rich sweet.

Atholl Brose

6 oz medium oatmeal (200 g)
4 dsp heather honey

1½ pt whisky (750 ml)
¼ pt water (150 ml)

Put the oatmeal into a small bowl and add water to make a paste. Leave for one hour, then put into a fine sieve and press all the liquid through. Add the honey to the sieved liquid and mix through. Pour into a large bottle and fill up with whisky. Shake well and always shake before use.

This is a celebration mixture and is consumed in large quantities at Hogmanay. It not only provides the necessary alcoholic stimulation but combines this with some welcome sustenance during the long nights of Highland festivities.

Gromack

1 tbsp oatmeal
1 tbsp honey

1 tbsp whisky
Cream to taste

Mix all the ingredients to a supping consistency and eat with a teaspoon from a glass.

This is a variation of Cromack which refers to the amount of meal held between the tips of the fingers and thumb. This mixture is often given to someone who has come in frozen and wet from the hill. It is very similar to the Atholl Brose mixture except for the cream and the fact that it is made up to order rather than kept in a bottle.

OATCAKES, BANNOCKS AND FARLES

In Celtic countries the name used for the staple item of food was not, as in other parts of Britain, Loaf. This was because they did not actually produce such an oven-baked, leavened article but instead made a flat, unleavened variety baked on a girdle. This was originally known as a 'Kaak of bread' in the days when bread meant a slice rather than the whole loaf. We still refer to a Loaf of Bread but the *kaak* has taken on quite different meanings. In oat*cakes* and also in the Scottish pan*cake*, however, it retains its original concept. When Scotland is referred to as the Land o' Cakes in literature it does not mean the land of the fancy, sweetened varieties we are familiar with today, but the simple, unleavened, unsweetened cake of bread or oatcake, since oats were the staple grain crop.

Bannocks were a home-made, unleavened form of bread which were always made thicker than an oatcake and in a large round or oval shape rather than cut into quarters. Barley was the commonest grain used for bannocks (see p. 51), though peasemeal, oatmeal, wheaten flour and the powdered silverweed root were also used.

A Farle or Farl was a quarter of an oatcake.

Highland Oatcakes

The secret of handling these oatcakes is to complete the process before the mixture cools too much, when it becomes brittle and very difficult to roll out thinly without breaking. Only enough to fill one girdle is made up at a time.

4 oz fine oatmeal (100 g)	Pinch of salt
¼ oz dripping or lard or butter (5 g)	Pinch of bicarbonate of soda
	Hot water to mix

Preheat the girdle – it should be nicely warm when you hold your hand about one inch from the surface.

Melt the fat in about 3–4 tbsp boiling water. Put the oatmeal into a bowl and make a well in the centre. Pour in the hot water and fat and mix to a stiff dough. Turn out onto a board dusted with oatmeal and quickly roll into a round about ¹/₈″ (3 mm) thick. Keep rubbing with dry oatmeal to prevent sticking.

Cut into quarters (farls) and bake slowly on the girdle till they harden and the corners begin to turn up at the edges. Originally they were then toasted slightly before a peat fire in a rack or toaster. Today they can be put into a cool oven for about half an hour. Store in an airtight tin. They are best heated slightly before use.

Highland Cakes

A very light, soft scone which should be eaten straight from the girdle.

8 oz self-raising flour (250 g)	1 egg
2 oz butter (50 g)	¼ pt hot milk (125 ml)

Preheat the girdle – it should feel fairly hot if you hold your hand over it about an inch from the surface.

Sift the flour into a bowl. Rub in butter. Make a well in the centre and add egg and milk to make a soft, elastic dough.

Turn out onto a floured board, dust on top with some flour and flour your hands. Press out very lightly with your hands to make a round about ½″ (1 cm) thick. Cut in half and lift both halves carefully onto the girdle. Cut into thirds or quarters and separate the cakes. Cook for about five minutes on either side. Place in a cloth on a cooling wrack. Eat warm with butter and jam or honey.

HOGMANAY – The New Year Festival
There was a time in Scotland when children expected Santa to come down the chimney on New Year's Eve rather than Christmas. Now this is as much a fading memory of bygone days as the communal gathering at market crosses in towns and cities throughout the country to welcome in the New Year. In rural areas traditions have a habit of persisting, and in the more remote and closely-knit communities of the Highlands and Islands, for example, Christmas often passes without much fuss. Cards and presents may be exchanged, but the day itself is often a normal one without any special eating or drinking.

As the New Year approaches, however, the housewife embarks on the preparations. A large joint of meat, usually a gigot of mutton or a haunch of venison, is cooked and left to cool. This is served cold in slices with oatcakes and butter. Vast quantities of shortbread are baked and finally on the Eve itself the dumpling is mixed and put on to boil. Neat whisky, Atholl Brose (see p. 105) and cups of tea are the sustaining drinks. The traditional way of drinking whisky is in a communal glass. When a group arrives at a house with their bottle one of the men takes 'the glass' round the company, filling it anew for each person and offering it with the season's greetings.

Cloutie Dumpling

1 lb plain flour (500 g)	1 tsp baking powder
6 oz breadcrumbs (175 g)	½ tsp salt
½ lb sultanas (250 g)	2 tsp each of cinnamon,
½ lb currants (250 g)	mixed spice and
4 oz raisins (125 g)	ginger

The name originates from the use of a cloth or clout *to boil the dumpling in. They are specially popular in the Highlands at Hogmanay when a giant-sized dumpling is produced to sustain people through the night. Recipes are seldom written down since it is strictly a rule-of-thumb affair and therefore no two dumplings ever taste the same. This is a fairly rich but not too heavy one. It is worth making a large one since its leftovers provide useful breakfasts fried with bacon. Slices may be wrapped in foil and heated through in the oven and served with cream for a pudding.*

4 oz chopped mixed peel (125 g)
$\frac{1}{2}$ lb brown sugar (250 g)
$\frac{1}{2}$ lb finely chopped suet (250 g)
2 grated cooking apples
2 grated carrots

$\frac{1}{2}$ lb black treacle (250 g)
2 eggs
Zest and juice of one orange or lemon
Milk to mix

Mix all the ingredients together in a large bowl, using the milk to mix to a soft consistency.

Half-fill a very large pot with water and bring to the boil. Add a large piece of cotton or linen cloth to the boiling water and leave in it for a few minutes. Lift out with some tongs, allow excess water to drip off then lay out. Sprinkle with a thin layer of flour to form a seal. Add the mixture, draw up the edges and tie up with some string leaving a little room for expansion.

Put a plate in the bottom of the pan and then add the dumpling. The water should come about $\frac{3}{4}$ of the way up the dumpling. Bring to simmering point, cover and cook for about 3 hours. Check the water level occasionally. The dumpling can also be boiled in a greased pudding bowl. Half the mixture will fill a 3 pt (1$\frac{1}{2}$ L) bowl. Cover the top with foil or greaseproof paper and tie securely. Check the water level occasionally to keep the level about half-way up the bowl.

To turn out dumpling and serve, fill up a basin with cold water and have ready a bowl that the dumpling will fit neatly into. Also a large, round, heated ashet or plate.

First dip the pudding into the cold water for one second only. This prevents the dumpling sticking to the cloth. Now put it into the bowl and loosen the string. Open out the cloth and hang over the sides of the bowl. Put the serving dish over the bowl, invert it and then remove the cloth carefully. Dry off in the oven or in front of a fire. Sprinkle with some caster sugar and eat hot with cream or custard.

Granny Loaf

This boiled fruit cake is very quick and easy to make and is really only a modern development of the Cloutie Dumpling. A large breakfast cup should be used (approx. 10 fl oz or 300 ml).

1 cup water
1 cup sugar
3 oz margarine (75 g)
1 tsp mixed spice
12 oz mixed fruit (350 g)

1 tsp bicarbonate of soda
2 eggs
1 cup self-raising flour
1 cup plain flour

Preheat the oven to 350°F/180°C or gas mark 4

Put the water, sugar, margarine, mixed spice and fruit into a pan and bring to the boil. Simmer for a few minutes and then leave to cool.

When quite cold, add the soda, eggs, and sifted flours. Turn into a greased loaf tin with a base $8\frac{1}{2}'' \times 4\frac{1}{2}''$ (21 cm × 11 cm). Bake in a moderate oven for $1\frac{1}{4}$ hours.

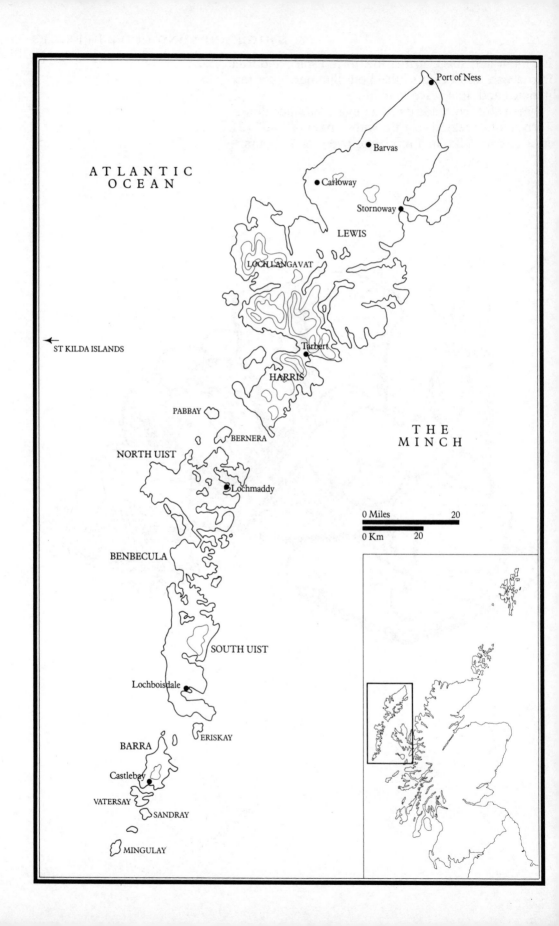

9. The Outer Hebrides

An intricate pattern of land and sea makes up this 130-mile-long barrier of islands which lies between the West Coast and the Atlantic Ocean. In many ways its history and origins are similar to the West Coast. It is a crofting, fishing community, originally self-sufficient with strong Celtic connections. It was, however, dominated by Norsemen for many centuries, which can be seen in place names, mostly round the coast, like Ness (*nes* – 'a headland'), Arnish ('Ari's ness'), Carloway ('Karli's bay'). Traces of Norse influence in the eating traditions are not so easy to find, though remnants of them must exist. It is more likely that remoteness, insularity and a distinct lack of natural resources have had more influence on the characters of the people and what they eat.

The fertile land is confined to limited areas round the coast, on the 'machair' and in a more extensive flat area of fertile land in the North of Lewis. More crofts are actively worked today in the Outer Hebrides than in any of the other crofting counties. Peat is the main source of fuel, found mostly inland, where huge slabs of bare rock worn smooth by the elements alternate with stretches of peat bog and innumerable lochans in a virtually treeless landscape.

ISLAND DIET

Fishing supplements the diet throughout the year, and the use of seaweed and shellfish has always been an important addition to the food supplies. On the sporting estates there are deer, but fishing is the main sporting activity, as numerous lochs and rivers teem with trout and salmon. On Lewis the river Grimersta which comes out of Loch Langavat ('Long Water' in Norse), though less than two miles long, is reputed to be the best salmon river in Europe.

As on the West Coast, a great deal of boiling is done: boiled mutton, fish, vegetables and puddings. This is also the land of Crappit Heads, Sheep's Head Broth, Salt Herring and potatoes and Cloutie Dumplings. The instinct to put food in a pot and add water is very strong and is found in all the areas where peat was the main source of heat and there was a poverty of resources. All baking was done on the girdle, the other piece of equipment which goes with a peat fire.

In the past people on these islands, stretched to the limits of their resources, were obliged to use everything that was available and therefore sea-birds and their eggs were often used for food. Puffins were made into soup with oatmeal. Cormorants were boiled till tender then sprinkled with brown sugar and a few cloves, covered with rashers of bacon and baked. Solan Goose (gannet) was also boiled till tender. This was the staple item of diet in St Kilda, where the people rowed over to the Stacks – islands about five miles away from the main island – to the nesting cliffs. They made the trip twice a year, in the spring and just before the fat young ones left the nests. They were salted down by the thousand and the eggs were eaten all through May and June.

Stornoway is the centre of the fishing industry in the islands with some herring landed but the catch is mostly white fish, lobsters, crabs, winkles, scallops, mussels and a great deal of prawns, otherwise known as Norwegian Lobsters or Dublin Bay Prawns.

Hebridean Shellfish

Shellfish	Butter
Seasoned flour	Bacon

Put shellfish in cold water, bring to the boil and cook till the shells open.

Remove flesh, dip in seasoned flour and fry lightly in butter. Serve with fried bacon.

Whelks in Sauce

Whelks	$\frac{1}{2}$ pt milk (250 ml)
1 oz flour (25 g)	$\frac{1}{2}$ pt cooking liquor
1 oz butter (25 g)	(250 ml)

Steep whelks in cold fresh water for at least 12 hours in a large pail with a lid, or you will find them all over the kitchen in no time. Drain and put in a pan of boiling salted water. Boil for about 10 minutes. Remove whelks from shells with a pin.

Melt the butter and add flour. Cook for a few minutes without browning, then add the liquid gradually. Bring to the boil and simmer for 5 minutes. Add whelks, season and serve with hot buttered toast.

Whelk Soup

$\frac{1}{2}$ lb whelks, cooked and	$\frac{1}{2}$ pt milk (300 ml)
picked out (225 g)	$\frac{1}{2}$ pt water (300 ml)
1 pt cooking liquor ($\frac{1}{2}$ L)	1 oz fine oatmeal (25 g)

Garnish –
Chopped parsley

Nearly all the shellfish is exported but some might find its way onto the dining tables of local hotels, in which case it would probably be cooked in a fairly elaborate way like the recipe for Lobster Hebridean (see p. 114). The island people have a much simpler method, as they have for cooking most foods; the lobsters are boiled and halved, then the meat is mixed with fresh cream and served in the shell. The Lewis way of cooking razor fish, scallops, clams, cockles and mussels is equally simple.

After the whelks have been cooked, leave the cooking liquid to settle and then gently decant 1 pint ($\frac{1}{2}$ L). Put into a pan and add milk and water. Bring to the boil and then sprinkle in oatmeal. Boil for about 20 minutes. Just before serving, add the whelks and parsley. Check seasoning and serve.

Lobsters

The lobster season lasts from April through to November. Lobsters should be 9″ (23 cm) long before they can be sold. The best weight is between 1$\frac{1}{2}$–2$\frac{1}{2}$ lbs (750–1250 g). If you are buying the lobster live, it should flap its tail when lifted and show some signs of life. When cooked, a sign of freshness is a good spring in the tail when you pull it out straight and let it go.

Lobster Hebridean

The flavour of Drambuie combines well with lobster in this dish. Although it does not have its origins in the island cuisine, it satisfies a need to refine and develop some dishes using local produce so that the Scottish gastronomic map may be extended a little.

2 lobsters live or cooked	1 oz butter (25 g)
2 oz butter (50 g)	1 small onion stuck with a few cloves and a Bay leaf
3–4 tbsp Drambuie	1 oz Dunlop cheese
$\frac{1}{4}$ pt double cream (150 ml)	Salt and pepper
Salt and pepper	*For the Garnish –*
For the cheese sauce –	8 oz mushrooms
$\frac{1}{2}$ pt milk (300 ml)	1 oz butter, melted
1 oz flour (25 g)	

If the lobsters are live, plunge them into a pan of boiling water, cover and simmer for 20 minutes. Remove them when the water has cooled a bit. Split the lobsters in half lengthwise with a large, sharp knife. Scissors may also be used, cutting through both sides of the shell then cutting through the flesh with a knife. This gives a good clean edge.

Remove the stomach sack at the top of the head. It is about 1″ long and $\frac{3}{4}$″ diameter (2.5 × 2 cm), depending on the size of the lobster. It will have split in two halves when you cut the lobster, so remove both halves and discard. Pull out and discard the blackish intestinal vein which runs right through the lobster, the greenish/blackish soft part (brain) should be scooped out and sieved into a small bowl.

Remove the meat from the tail sections, claws, claw joints, chest sections and legs. Pull off and discard the gills which are attached to the outside of the chest at the leg joints. Scrape out any white matter which has coagulated inside the shells and add to the brain. Cut the meat into approximately ½" (1 cm) pieces. Clean out the shells and put in a warm place with the serving dish.

To make the cheese sauce, simmer the onion, cloves and bay leaf in milk for 10–15 minutes. Meanwhile make up a white roux with butter and flour and leave to cool. Strain the milk and add gradually. Season and bring to the boil slowly, stirring all the time. Simmer for 10 minutes. Add the cheese at the end, mixing with a whisk until it is thoroughly melted and mixed through. Add sieved brain and check seasoning.

To make up the dish, melt the butter in a large frying pan. Add the lobster meat and toss for a few minutes. Sprinkle on the Drambuie and flame. When all the flames have died down, add the cheese sauce and cook for a few minutes. Then add the cream and heat through. Adjust the consistency if necessary and check the seasoning. Pour into the shells and garnish with grilled mushrooms and sprigs of parsley. Serve immediately.

Fried Cockles

Cockles   Salt and pepper
Butter

Place the cockles in fresh water and leave overnight. Rinse the cockles in fresh water. Place in a pan of boiling water and boil for a few minutes. Strain and shell.

Melt butter in a frying pan and toss cockles over a gentle heat for 2–3 minutes. Season with salt and pepper and serve.

These are collected from the beach where the plane lands on the island of Barra. A rake, with blunted points, is the best way of pulling them out of the sand since they are often about an inch or two below the surface. Don't use any which are less than 1" (2.5 cm) across.

Carrageen (Sea Moss)

This seaweed is found on the mid-tide line. It grows in clusters of purple-brown fronds. These have a distinctly flat stalk and branch repeatedly into a fan shape. It is usually gathered May–August when it is still young. If cooked when fresh, use one part by volume of carrageen to three parts of liquid (milk or water); otherwise the method is the same as for dried carrageen.

If you want to dry the weed it should be washed, then laid outside on a white cloth somewhere out of the wind. It has to be washed occasionally with fresh water or left in the rain. Eventually it will become bleached to a creamy-white colour. Make sure it is thoroughly dried off then put into paper bags and hang up in a dry place.

Commercially prepared dried carrageen is available

from health food shops or chemists. It usually has not had the sea-salt washed off and therefore has to be put into a bowl of hot water for a few seconds then drained before use. It is also used to thicken soups, stews, jams, jellies and marmalade. The cleaned carrageen is suspended in a muslin bag in the contents of the saucepan.

Carrageen Mould

1 oz carrageen (25 g)	Sugar to taste
2 pt milk (1 L)	

Hebrideans and other West Coast people eat this with no flavouring but with large quantities of fresh cream. They like to taste the sea-tang of the carrageen. In the Jelly recipe this is lost and the seaweed is used simply as a substitute for gelatine, but it makes a very good jelly.

Put the carrageen and milk into a pan, bring to the boil and simmer for 15–20 minutes. Strain. Add sugar, sometimes an egg is added at this stage, and pour into a mould to set. Serve with equal quantities of fresh double cream.

Carrageen Jelly

1½ pt water ($\frac{3}{4}$ L)	2 lemons
1 oz carrageen (25 g)	1 orange
6 oz sugar (175 g)	Green colouring

Put the carrageen and water into a large pot and bring to the boil. Add the zest of the lemons and orange. Cover and simmer for about 10 minutes.

Put the sugar into a 3-pint (1 L) glass dish and add the juice from the orange and lemons. When the carrageen is ready, strain over the sugar. Mix well to dissolve sugar and then add some green colouring. Set aside to cool and set. In a cool place this will take about ½ hour. Decorate with whipped cream and serve.

Pickled or Soused Mackerel

In this Harris recipe the brown sugar flavours the fish and darkens it slightly.

8 fresh mackerel fillets	Vinegar
Soft brown sugar	Water
Salt	

Spread a layer of fillets in a dish, flesh side uppermost. Sprinkle with some brown sugar and some salt. Cover with more fillets and continue with layers of sugar and salt. Leave overnight in a cool place.

Next day wash in cold water. Place fish in a pan and just cover with equal quantities of vinegar and water. Bring gradually to simmering point and simmer for 5 minutes. Leave to cool in the pickle and serve cold with a salad.

Fried Skate

2 lb wing of skate (1 kg) Salt and pepper
3 oz butter (75 g) Boiling salted water
Seasoned flour

Very large skate are to be found in these waters and this is the most common way of cooking them.

Soak skate overnight in cold water. Drain and cut into 4 portions. Put into boiling salted water and simmer for 5 minutes. Remove skin and bones and coat in seasoned flour. Melt the butter in a frying pan and fry the skate gently for a few minutes. Season and serve with the butter and boiled potatoes.

Port of Ness Cod

1½ lb cod, on the bone 2 oz butter (50 g)
 (750 g) 2–3 tbsp milk
Salt and pepper
2 lb potatoes, boiled and
 mashed (1 kg)

A simple way of cooking and serving cod.

Garnish –
Parsley

Put the cod into a pan and just cover with water. Season with salt and pepper and bring to the boil. Simmer for 2–5 minutes, depending on the thickness of the cod. Remove cod from the pan, skin and bone. Put flakes into a large heated ashet and put pats of butter on top. Moisten with a little of the cooking liquor and sprinkle liberally with chopped parsley. Add the milk and a little of the butter to the potatoes and cream them. Serve round the fish on the ashet.

Lewis way of frying Brown Trout

4 trout, about ½ lb each 2 oz seasoned oatmeal
 (250 g) (50 g)
Salt Oil or fat for frying
Milk

The small, speckled brown trout which are found in the many lochs, burns and rivers have a delicate sweet flavour.

After the trout have been gutted, salt them inside and out. Cover and leave in a cool place overnight. The next day, wipe the fish and split them open to remove the bone. Dip the fillets in milk and coat thickly in seasoned oatmeal. Heat oil or fat in frying pan and place in fillets flesh side down, turning once. They will only take a few minutes on either side. Serve with butter.

Often a special muslin bag is kept for boiling roes. They are eaten with great relish as a welcome variation in a fish diet.

Boiled Fish Roe

1 lb fish roe (500 g)	Salt and pepper
Cold water	½ lb bacon (250 g)

Wash roe and place on a piece of foil. Season and wrap up loosely or wrap in greaseproof paper and then tie in a cloth. Immerse in cold water and bring to the boil. Simmer for 20–30 minutes. Remove roe and serve hot with mashed potatoes and butter.
OR
Leave to cool, cut in ½″ (1 cm) slices and toss in seasoned flour. Fry in butter on both sides. Serve with fried bacon and fried potatoes.

Roe Cakes

1 lb cooked roe (500 g)	½ oz butter (15 g)
½ lb cooked potatoes (250 g)	Oil for frying
1 medium onion, finely chopped	Salt and pepper
	1 oz seasoned flour (25 g)

Melt the butter in a frying pan and cook the onion till it is soft and transparent, but not browned. Remove the skin from the roe. Mash the potatoes and roe together with a potato-masher and then add the onion and butter. Season.

Divide mixture into 8 pieces and, working on a floured board, shape the pieces into round cakes about ½″ (1 cm) thick using the flour to coat them and prevent sticking. Leave in a cool place for 1 hour before shallow frying in hot oil. Serve with fried bacon.

MUTTON AND BEEF

Sheep were kept in the Hebrides mainly for their wool. When they were killed, it was either by accident, disease or starvation. The neck and head were always used for a pot of broth; the legs were usually boiled with carrots and turnips. The stomach bag and innards were used to make the island version of a Haggis (Marag), while most of the larger joints of the carcass would have been salted. The meat was covered in fresh salt and left for about a fortnight. Then it was taken out of the pickle and hung up near or above a peat fire to dry. It was soaked overnight before use. The boned leg was known as a Mutton Ham.

Cattle were an important source of income and so they were seldom eaten. Sometimes they were bled, if times were hard, and a blood pudding made (Marag Dubh). But, like mutton, the carcass would have been salted. The Hough (lower leg, known in England as Shin) was made into Potted Hough and was also used for soup.

Kale Soup

2 lb hough (1 kg)	Water
4 oz barley (100 g)	Salt and pepper
1 lb kale (500 g)	

Cut up the hough fairly finely and put into a pan with the water and bring to the boil. Skim, add barley, salt and pepper and simmer for 2–3 hours. About 20 minutes before it is ready add the kale finely chopped. Check seasoning and serve.

Lewis Kailkenny

1 lb potatoes, cooked (500 g)	1 lb cabbage, cooked (500 g)
1 lb carrots, cooked (500 g)	2½ fl oz cream (75 ml)
	Salt and pepper

Mash potatoes, carrots and cabbage and beat in cream. Season. Serve hot or make into cakes and fry.

The range of vegetables on the islands is not extensive. Three of them combine in this recipe, making a dish which would have been considered a main meal in its original form.

Peat-roast Potatoes

Potatoes of an equal size	Butter
Red hot peat ashes	Salt

Wash potatoes and dry. Place in hot ashes till cooked. Remove top, put in knob of butter. Eat with a teaspoon, adding salt as required.

This is a popular way of cooking potatoes, as the gentle heat from the peat cooks them slowly and flavours the potatoes at the same time.

OTHER HEBRIDEAN DELICACIES

Sweet Maragan

½ lb flour (250 g)	Salt and pepper
½ lb oatmeal (250 g)	2 oz sugar (50 g)
4 oz suet, finely chopped (125 g)	1 tsp onion, diced
	2 oz raisins (50 g)

Mix all the ingredients together in a bowl and add enough water to bind them together without making the mixture wet. Put into a floured pudding cloth or a

This is similar to the Ayrshire Sweet Haggis (see p. 47) but is heavier and less crumbly since there is more flour in this one.

greased 2 pt (1 L) pudding bowl and steam or boil gently for 2–3 hours. Serve hot or it may also be served in slices when cold, fried up with potatoes and bacon.

Greiseagan

'Little black berries found on moors' were used for this dish which is an island version of Skirlie without the onions. The berries used originally were black bear-berries; when they were not available currants were used instead.

Suet, chopped
Currants or raisins or blaeberries

Oatmeal
(Quantities to taste)

Fry the suet in a pan till crisp. Then add currants, raisins or blaeberries and oatmeal, stir and cook gently for 5–10 minutes.

Barley Bannocks

Barley flour adds a distinctive flavour to the bannocks. It can be bought from health food shops or grain stores. Some bakers in Stornoway still sell these bannocks.

½ lb barley flour (225 g)
2 oz plain flour (50 g)
1 tsp cream of tartar

½ tsp salt
½ pt buttermilk (250 ml)
1 tsp bicarbonate of soda

Preheat the girdle – it should feel nicely warm if you hold your hand over it about an inch from the surface.

Sift the barley flour, flour, cream of tartar and salt into a bowl. Add the soda to the buttermilk. Stir in. Make a well in the centre of the flour and add the buttermilk. Lightly make into a soft dough and turn out onto a floured board. Flour the top and press out with your hand to make a round about ½″ thick. Cut into quarters or sixths and bake on a hot girdle. Turn and brown on the other side. Wrap up in a cloth to keep them soft.

Bonnach Imeach

This Hebridean oatcake is quite different from the thin, crisp West Highland variety. It has more 'body', is thicker, heavier and much less brittle. The Gaelic name means 'cake with butter'.

12 oz medium oatmeal (350 g)
½ oz butter (15 g)

1 egg
4 fl oz hot milk (100 ml)

Preheat the girdle as for Barley Bannocks.

Put the oatmeal into a bowl, add salt and rub in butter. Make a well in the centre and add the egg and milk. Mix to a fairly stiff dough. Roll out to ¼″ (½ cm) into a large round cut into triangles (12) and bake for about 5 minutes on both sides on a hot girdle. Cool and serve with butter and honey or cheese.

10. Orkney and Shetland

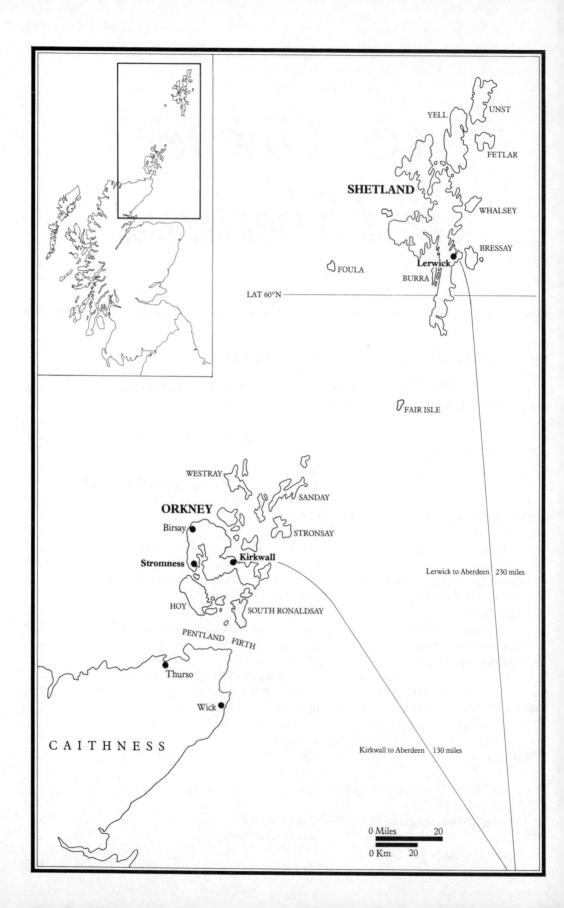

UNST

YELL

FETLAR

SHETLAND

WHALSEY

BRESSAY

FOULA

Lerwick

BURRA

LAT 60°N

FAIR ISLE

WESTRAY

SANDAY

ORKNEY

STRONSAY

Birsay

Stromness   Kirkwall

HOY

SOUTH RONALDSAY

PENTLAND FIRTH

Thurso

Wick

CAITHNESS

Lerwick to Aberdeen   230 miles

Kirkwall to Aberdeen   130 miles

0 Miles   20

0 Km   20

These two regions are so often linked together it might be assumed that there are many similarities between them. There are some – the fact that they are both groups of islands and were both originally crofting-fishing communities and they were both invaded and ruled by Norsemen for many centuries. But in the differing nature of their land and its produce they do not belong naturally together.

The gentle, undulating, green and fertile land of the Orkneys has more in common with the North-East Lowlands of Morayshire, Easter Ross and Caithness than with Shetland. This is fine farming country for rearing cattle, sheep and pigs as well as growing oats, barley and turnips. In Shetland, acid soils, a cool summer and frequent salt-laden gales restrict farming so that the people have turned much more towards the sea for a living than in Orkney. In this respect they belong more with the Hebrides and the West Coast. They were originally described as fishermen who had a croft, compared with the Orcadians who were farmers who kept a fishing boat. There are nearly four times as many fishermen in Shetland as there are in Orkney, but on the other hand Orkney farms are four times the size of those in Shetland.

THE ORKNEYS

The independently progressive and hard-working Orcadians have reaped a considerable harvest from their land. Grass is the main crop which the cattle graze on in the long summer days and which is cut for hay and silage for winter feeding. The main breed of beef cattle is Aberdeen Angus with Friesians and Ayrshires the mainstay of the dairying industry. There are fifteen times as many beef cattle and twice as many dairy cattle as in Shetland. The number of sheep is on the decline since they are not as profitable as cattle. Pigs and poultry have always been an important item of diet. In 1814 John Shirreff commented in his *General View of The Agriculture of the Orkney and Shetland Islands* that in Orkney – 'people prefer pig to any other meat'. They cured the meat by making hams and today there is still a flourishing industry in bacon and pig products which is a typical adjunct to a dairying area.

ORKNEY CHEESE

In 1812, according to John Shirreff, the farmers had a visit from two Ayrshire dairywomen who taught them 'the mode of making the Dunlop or Ayrshire cheese'. From this technique, applied to the distincive milk of the country which depends for its flavour on the quality of the pasture and the breed of the cow, there developed the traditional Orkney cheese. Three-and-a-half million gallons of milk are now processed every year into Orkney cheese and butter in large modern creameries at Kirkwall and Birsay.

The cheese-making methods at the creameries have been copied from the farmhouse and adapted to factory conditions, but the highly individualistic farmhouse cheese-making has not entirely died out and its products can often be bought in some shops in Kirkwall. Since these home-made farm cheeses take their flavour from the pastures and the cows, and are also dependent for flavour and texture on the cheese-maker's technique, they are unique local products and greatly esteemed. Cheese was a staple item of the Orkney diet in the past and was always kept buried in oatmeal to prevent it drying out.

ORKNEY LOBSTERS AND SMOKED SALMON

Although fishing comes second to farming for the Orcadians, they have for many years supplied lobsters to markets in Paris, London and Scandinavia, and the high prices fetched for this catch have supplemented the income of many a small farm. During the summer, when lobsters are out of season, many shellfish boats concentrate on catching crabs which are becoming more popular.

In Kirkwall a fish-curing business has developed a process for smoking salmon which has made an international reputation, and people send salmon from all over the world for the special Orkney cure.

OTHER ORKNEY RECIPES

In this rich dairying area with its milk and pork adjuncts such dishes as Pork and Kale, Clapshot, Oatmeal Soup and Tatties and Cream are a natural development.

Baking specialities are mostly of the girdle variety and bakers' shops here have an enormous selection. Most interesting perhaps are the Bere Bannocks which are made with beremeal. Bere is a northern form of barley which makes a delicious dark greyish coloured bannock with a full nutty flavour quite distinctive from other varieties.

Orkney Pork and Kale

½ oz butter or oil (15 g)
12 oz streaky or back
    bacon (375 kg)
2 lb potatoes (1 kg)
2½ lb cabbage (1¼ kg)

Water
Salt and freshly-ground
    black pepper
1 dsp dill seeds

Melt butter or oil in a large pot. Chop up the bacon roughly and add to the pot. Fry gently for a few minutes till the bacon is crisp.

Peel and slice the potatoes about ¼″ (½ cm) thick. Chop up the cabbage fairly finely. Add these to the pot, season and mix in well. Cover and cook gently for about 5 minutes, stirring occasionally. Add enough water to come about ½″ (1 cm) up the pan. Sprinkle dill seeds on top, bring up to simmering point, cover, and cook gently till the potatoes are cooked. Check occasionally to make sure it is not sticking. Check seasoning and serve hot.

Kale is used here in its loosest sense, meaning any kind of greens. Cabbages in Orkney were originally a variety known as Kilmaurs Kale and were a dusky reddish hue. They are combined here in one of the staple dishes which was originally made with a piece of pickled pork. This modern version is more like Orcadian Stovies. The Scandinavian use of dill seeds adds an interesting flavour to the dish.

Clapshot

1 lb potatoes, boiled
    (500 g)
1 lb turnip, boiled
    (500 g)

1 oz chives (25 g)
1 oz butter or dripping
    (25 g)
Salt and pepper

Mash together potatoes and turnips. Add chives and dripping or butter. Season and serve very hot.

This is one of the best-known Orkney dishes, though the origin of the name is obscure. It very often accompanies haggis.

Orcadian Oatmeal Soup

2 oz butter (50 g)
2 medium-sized carrots,
    grated
1 leek, chopped
6 oz turnip or cabbage,
    finely chopped (175 g)

1 oz fine oatmeal (25 g)
1 pt stock (½ L)
¾ pt milk (375 ml)
Salt and pepper

Melt the butter in a large pot and add all the vegetables. Stir with a wooden spoon and reduce to a low heat. Cover and cook very gently for about 5 minutes, stirring occasionally. Add the oatmeal and stir in. Cook for another 5 minutes. Then add the stock and salt and pepper and simmer for about 15 minutes. The soup can be liquidised or sieved at this point. Add milk just before serving. Heat through and check the seasoning. Serve.

A quick, easy and very good vegetable soup which brings out the flavour of the vegetables. It is only very slightly thickened with oatmeal.

Tatties and Cream

In this rich dairy area cream is used here with the potatoes to make an original potato dish which might be served as a main meal with some Farmhouse Orkney Cheese.

2 lb new potatoes (1 kg)
2 oz butter (50 g)
1 medium onion, finely chopped
¼ pt single cream (125 ml)

1 tbsp chopped parsley
1 tbsp chopped mint
Salt and pepper

Boil potatoes, drain, peel and dice. Melt butter in a pan and add onion. Cook till transparent but not browned. Add potatoes, cream, parsley and mint and heat through. Season and serve.

Fatty Cutties

These are similar to the Northumbrian Singin' Hinnies which had so much fat in them they sizzled or 'sang' as they cooked on the girdle.

6 oz plain flour (175 g)
Pinch of bicarbonate of soda
3 oz granulated sugar (75 g)

3 oz currants (75 g)
3 oz melted margarine (75 g)

Preheat the girdle – it should feel fairly hot when you hold your hand about an inch from the surface.

Sift the flour and soda together in a bowl. Then mix in the currants and sugar. Now add the melted margarine and mix together to make a stiff dough.

Turn out onto a floured board and knead lightly till smooth. Divide into two equal pieces and roll out into a round about ¼" (½ cm) thick. Cut each circle into 4 or 6 triangles and cook on a hot girdle for about 5 minutes on each side till they are nicely browned. Serve the same day as they are baked.

Sour Skons

The sweet caraway flavour combines with the sharp tang of the oatmeal and buttermilk mixture which has been steeped for several days to produce this unique scone.

½ lb fine oatmeal (225 g)
½ pt buttermilk (250 ml)
½ lb plain flour (225 g)

1 tsp bicarbonate of soda
3 oz caster sugar (75 g)
1 dsp caraway seeds

Preheat the girdle – it should feel fairly hot if you hold your hand over it about an inch from the surface.

Put the oatmeal into a bowl, add buttermilk and mix well. Leave in a cool place for two or three days.

Sift the flour and soda onto the oatmeal and buttermilk mixture and then add the sugar and caraway seeds. Mix to a soft, elastic dough with a little more buttermilk. Turn onto a floured board and dust the top with flour. Handle as little and as lightly as possible, shaping into two rounds about ¾″ thick (2 cm). Divide each round into four and bake on a hot girdle for 5–10 minutes on either side. Wrap in a cloth and cool on a cooling rack.

Orkney Pancakes

6 oz fine oatmeal (175 g)	2 tbsp syrup
½ pt buttermilk or soured milk (250 ml)	1 tsp baking soda
3 oz self-raising flour (75 g)	1 egg
	Milk to mix

These are a variation of Scottish pancakes but made with oatmeal and buttermilk.

Preheat the girdle – it should feel fairly hot if you hold your hand over it about an inch from the surface.

Put the oatmeal into a bowl and add the buttermilk or milk that has been soured with a few tsp of lemon juice. Mix through, cover and leave overnight.

The next day sift in flour and soda. Stir in syrup, egg and then add enough milk to make a fairly thin consistency. Cook in spoonfuls on a hot girdle, browning on both sides. Cool in a cloth on a cooling rack.

Serve warm with butter and honey or syrup.

Orkney Broonies

8 oz fine oatmeal (225 g)	2 tsp ground ginger
4 oz self-raising flour (100 g)	4 oz margarine or butter (100 g)
5 oz golden syrup (150 g)	½ tsp bicarbonate of soda
2 oz black treacle (50 g)	¼ pt buttermilk (125 ml)
4 oz soft brown sugar (100 g)	1 egg
	Pinch of salt

These are unlike the Shetland version and more similar in many ways to a Yorkshire Parkin. They should be left to mature for at least a week in an airtight tin.

Preheat the oven to 350°F/180°C or gas mark 4

Mix the meal and flour together and rub in butter. Add salt, sugar, ginger and soda.

Mix the treacle, syrup, egg and buttermilk together and add to the dry ingredients to make a soft consistency. Pour into a lined 8″ (20 cm) square tin and bake for 35 minutes.

THE SHETLANDS

Lerwick is twenty miles nearer to Bergen than it is to Aberdeen. This isolation from mainland Scotland and relative proximity to Norway has produced a long history of Norse colonisation and culture in these islands, some of which can still be seen in the food traditions. There are other activities such as the celebrating of Yule rather than Christmas as the feast of the winter solstice and the Up-Helly-Aa ritual of burning a viking ship, celebrating the end of Yule and the dark hungry days of winter.

The need to preserve supplies of food by salting or drying for these long, hard winter months no longer applies today, but the methods of preservation which the Shetlanders used are similar to Scandinavian ones and unlike any of the other methods in Scotland.

They both shared a palate for the very strong flavour of fermented fish. In Sweden the best example of this which still survives today is the sour Baltic Herring or *Surstromming*. It is made with fresh herring which are salted in brine for one day then cleaned and packed into barrels. They are left in the sun for about twenty-four hours to get the fermentation process started and then put into a cool storage room to let fermentation continue at a slower rate. Ripe *Surstromming* is eaten with very thin, hard bread and boiled potatoes.

In Shetland, the young coal-fish – saith, gutted and washed in sea water and left in the open to ferment for eight to ten days – were known as *Sookit Piltaks*. Skate was buried in the ground for a considerable period, no doubt producing a similarly highly-flavoured product as a result. Also fish heads, or a small fish rolled in a cloth, were left in an airy place often between the stones in a wall and known as *Klossed Heads*.

Orkney and Shetland both share with Scandinavia extensive use of cabbage in their diet. It was fed to cattle and added to broths or eaten boiled with butter, but, in common with their palate for highly-developed fish cures, they also had a method of preserving cabbage which produced a highly-flavoured result. The chopped cabbage was packed into kegs (wooden barrels holding up to ten gallons) with layers of animal fat, oatmeal, salt and spices. A weight was put on top to press it down. When required, a piece was cut out and boiled to make a 'tasty and nourishing' soup.

FISHING

Shetland fishermen were pioneers of the fishing industry, bringing rich catches from the Faroes, Iceland and the North Sea long before the first decked vessels took up deep-sea fishing about 1856. Their proximity to these fishing grounds meant that they were not only able to export quantities of dried and salted fish but there were also abundant supplies for the people and as a result many original dishes developed. As well as quantity there was also variety in the fish available. Among the white fish cod, haddock, whiting, ling and tusk, as well as plaice and sole. Saith was an inshore fish which was caught and eaten all the year round. A *Sillock* was a young saith, a *Piltak* or *Piltock* a two-year-old one. Herring and mackerel were plentiful, the herring salt-pickled and latterly made into kippers.

Because there were always abundant and varied supplies of fish, shellfish were used as bait rather than for eating, and seaweed was not eaten a great deal, although the islanders make a milk jelly with carrageen.

LIVERS, ROES AND HEADS

More than in any other area, the innards of the fish were eaten in Shetlands. People were not in the habit of throwing away anything and, since large quantities of white fish, like cod, were salted and dried for winter use, the livers, roes and heads were a by-product of the salting industry and were used in many original ways.

The oil from fish liver was burnt in oil lamps, but it was also used in cooking instead of other fats. Sometimes the fish and its liver were simply boiled together and eaten with lots of potatoes (*Gree'd Fish*) or it was mixed with meal and onions as in the Highlands and the Hebrides and used to stuff the head (*Krappit Heed*) or the stomach (*Krappit Muggies*). The same mixture of meal and liver was made into dumplings which were cooked in boiling, salted water or on top of a stew or fish soup.

Shetlanders also made a kind of pie called *Liver-Krus* which was made with a stiff dough of wholemeal flour and water. This was shaped rather like a raised pie the size of a cup and then the pastry was filled with chopped fish livers and a lattice-design arranged on top. Traditionally they were set on the hearth beside the fire to bake since this was the nearest to roasting that this peat-burning cuisine came.

The fish liver was also used in making bannocks, the raw livers mixed through the meal. The bannocks were either eaten on their own or with fish.

Roes were usually boiled in a muslin bag then fried in butter or made into *Slott*. This seems to have been one of those recipes which varied from one household to another, but basically it was made with cod roe, beaten till creamy with some flour and sometimes a bit of ling liver. The mixture was dropped in spoonfuls into boiling seawater and eaten hot or, when cold, sliced and fried in butter.

Shetland Fish Soup

This always had a large head added for extra flavour.

1 cod head	$\frac{1}{4}$ pt milk (125 ml)
$\frac{1}{2}$ lb filleted white fish (250 g)	1 tsp salt
	Water
2 carrots, finely diced	
1 medium onion or leek, finely chopped	

Put the fish and head into a pan and cover with water. Add salt and bring to a gentle simmer. Cook for about 15 minutes then add the vegetables and cook for about another 30 minutes. Just before serving, remove the cod head and return the flesh from the head to the soup. Add the milk, check seasoning and serve.

Flats

These fish have a more delicate flavour and texture than other white fish so this simple steaming method is an ideal way of keeping the fish intact and preserving all the flavour at the same time.

Plaice, Sole, flounder, and dab	Salt
	Butter

Put the fish on a plate over a pan of boiling water. Season with salt and add a little butter. Cover the plate and cook the fish in its own juices.

Fried Herring and Onions

The onion and herring combination is a common Scandinavian one. This recipe demonstrates the links in that direction rather than with the rest of Scotland, where herring were usually coated in oatmeal rather than fried with onions.

8 fresh herring fillets	Seasoned flour
$\frac{1}{2}$ lb onion, sliced (250 g)	Butter for frying

Coat the fish in the flour. Melt the butter in a frying pan and fry the onions till they are golden brown. Remove and add herring. Fry on both sides for about 4–5 minutes and serve with the onions.

BEEF, MUTTON AND PORK

The traditional time for selling or killing cattle, sheep and pigs was at harvest time, just before the winter set in and feeding for animals became scarce. The carcasses were shared between families and all the parts were used. This was the time for salting and drying the meat and for making puddings with the entrails.

Joints were hung up to dry in special stone larders, built so that the air could blow freely through the walls, or it was kept fresh for many weeks, 'hung up in any cave into which the tide flows'. Wind-dried meat is known as *Vivda*.

Sassermaet and Brönies

1 lb minced beef (500 g)	A large pinch of the
1 oz breadcrumbs (25 g)	following –
1 egg	Mixed spice, freshly
1 small onion, finely	ground black pepper,
chopped	white pepper, ground
Seasoning mixture –	cloves and cinnamon
1 level dsp salt	Oil or butter for frying

Put the minced beef, breadcrumbs, egg and onions into a large bowl. Make up the seasoning mixture and mix with all the other ingredients.

Put some flour onto a board. Divide the mixture into 4 and shape into round patties 1" (2½ cm) thick, coating with flour to prevent them sticking.

Melt oil or butter in a frying pan and fry them gently for 5–10 minutes on both sides. Serve with some warm bannocks.

The Sassermaet mixture is a kind of preserved beef mince. About 6 lb (3 kg) of mince is spiced and salted and kept in a cool place. This is used with an equal quantity of fresh mince, breadcrumbs and onions and made into cakes and fried; it is then known as Brönies. The following recipe has been adapted to combine the two processes.

SHETLAND SHEEP

The Shetland sheep are different from other breeds in Britain and have more in common with Norwegian, Swedish and Russian breeds which resemble the wild sheep of Siberia. It is a small, hardy, self-reliant sheep which lives mostly on exposed hills, feeding on coarse hill grass and heather but in severe times it also feeds on seaweed from the shore. All this combines to produce a mutton with a unique flavour which is stronger and faintly gamey compared with lowland mutton.

The Shetland lamb is born from May onwards and they become available during a short period in October and November. Because of its unique flavour, simple roasting and grilling methods are best and highly-flavoured sauces such as mint should be avoided.

Roast Leg of Shetland Lamb

3 lb leg of lamb (1½ kg)	2 oz butter (50 g)
2–3 sprigs of fresh	2 lb medium to large
rosemary	potatoes (1 kg)
Salt and freshly ground	
black pepper	

Garnish –
Chopped parsley

This method is not traditional since sheep in Shetland were kept for their wool for the knitting industry and as a result were only killed when very old and tough. Allow 8 oz (250 g) of lamb on the bone per person. This recipe will serve 6.

Preheat the oven to 450°F/230°C or Gas mark 8

Prepare the lamb. Make some incisions with a sharp knife, sliding it in under the fat all over the skin and push the rosemary leaves into the slits.

Cut the potatoes into $\frac{1}{4}$–$\frac{1}{2}''$ ($\frac{1}{2}$–1 cm) slices and place in a 2" (5 cm) deep roasting tin or ovenproof dish about 11" × 9" (28 × 23 cm). Overlap the slices, making a good thick base for the lamb. Melt the butter and pour it over the potatoes. Turn them thoroughly and then season. Place the lamb on top and brush it liberally with the remaining butter. Season with salt and freshly ground black pepper.

Roast in a hot oven for 10 minutes to brown the meat then reduce to 350°F/180°C or gas mark 4, allowing 20 minutes per lb plus 20 minutes.

Turn the lamb and potatoes twice during the cooking so that they brown evenly. When ready, leave for 20 minutes in a warm place before carving to allow the juices to settle. Also the meat will be easier to carve. Serve with the potatoes garnished with parsley. The easiest way of serving is to use an ovenproof dish for the roasting which can then be taken to the table. Otherwise transfer to a heated ashet.

Boiled Mutton

A more traditional way of cooking mutton rather than lamb.

2 lb best end of neck or gigot (1 kg)	8 small new potatoes or 4 large, halved
2–3 carrots	4 pts water (2 L)
2 large onions, finely chopped	1 tsp salt
5 oz turnip (150 g)	2 tsp sugar

Put the water, sugar and salt into a large pan and bring to the boil. Put in meat, skim and simmer for 1 hour.

Cut the carrots into spears and cut the turnip into 1" (2.5 cm) cubes and add to the pot with the onion. Cook for another 30 minutes till both the meat and vegetables are tender.

To serve, remove the meat and cut into thick slices. Remove potatoes, carrots and turnips and serve with the meat. Add a little of the broth to moisten. Garnish with parsley. Serves 8–10.

Serve the broth the next day garnished with parsley. Any leftover meat can be diced and returned to the pot.

Boiled Pork

2½ lb salt-cured pork, collar, forehock or gammon (1¼ kg)
4 oz brown sugar (100 g)
Water

Put the joint into a very large pan. Cover with cold water and bring to the boil. Add brown sugar, cover and simmer for 30 minutes per lb plus 30 minutes.

Cool in the liquid overnight. Next day remove and cut off the skin. Dust with wholemeal flour and serve cold with a salad.

A local way of cooking pork in sugar. A kind of sweet porridge was made with the stock thickened with oatmeal or wholemeal flour and called Laverin.

Lentil Brö

8 oz lentils (250 g)
2 oz barley (50 g)
2 large onions, finely chopped
1 carrot, diced
½ medium turnip, diced
4 pt ham stock (2 L)
2 oz butter (50 g)

Melt butter in a large pot and add lentils, barley, onions, carrot, turnip, salt and pepper. Stir for a minute then cover and leave to cook gently for about 10 minutes, stirring occasionally.

Add stock, bring to the boil and simmer for 1–1½ hours. Check seasoning, garnish with parsley and serve with Barley bannocks (see p. 120) and butter.

The stock from the previous recipe can also be used in this soup.

Gooseberry Sauce

½ lb cooked gooseberries (250 g)
3 oz butter (75 g)
1 tbsp sugar

Melt the butter and sugar. Sieve or purée the gooseberries in a liquidiser. Add to the butter and boil for a few minutes. Serve hot.

It is practically impossible for trees to grow successfully on such a windswept landscape and so fruit trees are not common, but rhubarb, gooseberries and blaeberries were included in the diet. This sauce was served with pork and fried or grilled mackerel.

Potatoes with milk

1½ lb potatoes (750 g)
¾ pt milk (400 ml)
Salt and pepper

Preheat the oven to 350°F/180°C or gas mark 4

Peel and slice potatoes, put in a 2–2½ pt (1–1½ L) fire-proof dish. Add pepper and salt to the milk and pour over the potatoes. Cook in a moderate oven for 1½ hours, when they will be soft and nicely browned on top. Eat with fish.

Potatoes were introduced to the islands in the 18th century and have been an integral part of the diet ever since. They combine well with the oily fish dishes and also with dairy products as in this recipe.

Bride's Bonn or Bridal Cake

By tradition this was broken over the bride's head as she entered her new house for the first time as a married woman. It should be made and eaten in the same day.

5 oz self-raising flour (150 g)	2 oz butter (50 g)
1 oz caster sugar (25 g)	½ tsp caraway seeds
	milk to mix

Preheat the girdle – it should feel fairly hot if you hold your hand over it about one inch from the surface.

Sift the flour into a bowl and rub in the butter. Add sugar and caraway. Mix with milk to make a soft elastic dough. Place on a floured board, dust some flour on top and flour your hands well. Press out lightly to a round about ¾" (2 cm) thick. Divide into four triangles and put on a hot girdle. Bake for about 5 minutes on both sides. Cool in a cloth on a cooling rack.

Brunnies

The name comes from the Norwegian word brun, *meaning 'brown'.*

8 oz finely ground wholewheat flour (250 g)	1¼ tsp cream of tartar
½ tsp salt	Buttermilk to mix (For sweet milk use 2 tsp baking powder for raising agent)
1 tsp sugar	
1 tsp bicarbonate of soda	

Preheat the girdle – it should feel fairly hot when you hold your hand one inch from the surface.

Put all the dry ingredients into a bowl and mix them together. Make a well in the centre and add buttermilk. Mix to a soft dough. Turn out onto a floured board, dust some flour on top and roll out to ½" (1 cm) thick. Cut into 6 or 8 triangles and bake on a hot girdle on both sides for about 5–10 minutes on each side. Wrap in a cloth and put on a cooling rack.

Brunnies of Rye

Substitute 4 oz (125 g) of rye flour and add 1 tbsp of treacle and ½ oz (12 g) of melted butter.

Whipkull or Whipcol

An ancient Shetland drink which appears once a year at Yule time. It is taken at the end of the special Yule breakfast with a piece of rich, crisp shortbread. This is another food

4 egg yolks	3 tbsp rum
4 oz sugar (125 g)	

Put the sugar into a double boiler (or into a bowl over a pan of hot water), add the egg yolks and heat up the water in the bottom pan.

Beat the yolks and sugar till thick and creamy with a whisk or an electric beater. Then start to add the rum one tbsp at a time beating all the time. When it is all added, beat for another few minutes and then pour into wine glasses.

Serve it immediately when it is still warm, or chill for a few hours. It is very good served with a piece of Balmoral Shortbread (see p. 79).

tradition which Shetland shares with Norway rather than the rest of Scotland. Norwegians make exactly the same mixture and call it Eggedosis. *Sometimes it is served alone in a chilled dish or it accompanies a mixture of fresh fruits and is eaten as a kind of sauce. Italians make the same thing with Marsala and call it* Zabaglione.

GIRDLE BAKING AND BUTTERMILK

A Scots girdle is usually about 14″ (35 cm) in diameter and made of cast iron. More modern ones are a lighter aluminium, but in neither case should the surface ever be washed. A wipe with a dry cloth is usually all that is necessary, but it can be rubbed with some coarse salt and then dusted with a clean cloth. To prepare the surface for a batter, such as pancakes, it should be greased very lightly. The traditional way is to wrap a piece of beef suet in a piece of muslin and rub this over the surface when the girdle is hot. Some oil or lard can be rubbed in with a piece of cloth kept specially for the purpose. It is best to do this when the girdle is hot so that you use as little as possible. For scones and bannocks and anything that is dough rather than a batter, the surface should be dusted lightly with flour. When heating the girdle a slow, gentle heat over a long period gives an even temperature over the whole surface which is important if the baking is to be cooked evenly.

The use of buttermilk in the recipes for girdle baking is not vital but it does produce a particular type of scone or bannock which is bulkier, softer and moister than that made with fresh milk or soured milk. The flavour is also sharper. Cultured buttermilk is produced commercially and is fairly readily available. Milk which has just turned sour can be used instead, or fresh milk can be soured with some lemon juice. About 2–3 tsp to ½ pt (250 ml) of milk.

135

For American Readers:

EQUIVALENT MEASURES

There are some old British cooking terms and customs which are no longer in current use in Britain but which America still retains. The American pint, for instance, still has our pre-1825 system of measurement when the liquid pint was 16 oz and the equivalent of the imperial pound. Today, most American measuring for cooking is done by volume with a 8 fl oz cup rather than weighed on scales as it is in Britain.

The word *broil* was used in Britain up to the turn of the century, though we now say 'grill' instead. *Skillets* were also common in nineteenth-century recipes but we now refer to 'frying pans' while a kettle in Britain is something you boil water in and not a pan for stewing, which is the original meaning. The only remnant of this use is in the term *fish kettle*, a specially-shaped long pot for cooking a large whole fish like a salmon.

Here are some other variations between the two countries in measures, cooking terms, commodities and equipment.

EQUIVALENT MEASURES

Ingredients	British	American
Almonds, flaked	2 oz	½ cup
ground	2 oz	½ cup
blanched whole	2 oz	½ cup
Breadcrumbs, fresh	4 oz	2 cups
Butter or Broad beans (Lima)	8 oz	1½ cups
Crowdie, cottage or cream cheese	8 oz	1 cup
Cheese, grated	1 oz	¼ cup
Dried fruit, sultanas, currants, etc.	8 oz	1½ cups

Flour	8 oz	2½ cups
Glacé (candied) cherries	4 oz	¾ cup
Golden Syrup (Light corn syrup)	6 oz	½ cup
Liquid, milk, water etc.	1 pt	2½ cups
Mince (ground beef, hamburger)	8 oz	2 cups
Oatmeal, fine, medium	8 oz	2 cups
pinhead (Irish)	8 oz	2¼ cups
Rice	3 oz	½ cup
Solid fats, butter, margarine etc.	8 oz	1 cup
Suet	4 oz	1 cup
Sugar, granulated, caster	8 oz	1¼ cups
icing (powdered)	8 oz	1¾ cups
soft brown	8 oz	1¼ cups
Treacle (molasses)	8 oz	¾ cup

COOKING TERMS

British	American
Blood heat	Lukewarm
Fry	Pan Broil (without fat) or Pan Fry (with a little fat)
Grate	Shred
Grill	Broil
Gut	Clean
Knock back	Punch down
Prove	Rise
Sieve	Sift
Whisk	Beat, whip

COMMODITIES

Anchovy essence	Anchovy paste
Bannock	Flat, round cakes
Bicarbonate of soda	Baking soda
Biscuits	Cookies or crackers
Blaeberries	Bilberries
Boiling fowl	Stewing fowl
Broad beans	Lima beans
Cake mixture	Cake batter
Caster sugar	Granulated sugar
Cornflour	Cornstarch
Creamed potatoes	Mashed potatoes
Dessicated coconut	Flaked coconut
Double cream	Whipping cream

British	American
Dripping	Meat dripping
Essence	Extract
Farls, Farles	Quarters
Filleted fish	Fish fillets
Flaked almonds	Slivered almonds
Glacé	Candied
Golden syrup	Light corn syrup
Haricot beans	Navy beans
Hough	Shank of beef
Icing	Frosting
Jam or Jelly	Preserves or Jelly
Jelly (sweet)	Gelatin dessert
Mince	Hamburger or Ground
Pinhead oatmeal	Irish oatmeal
Plain flour	All-purpose flour
Rasher	Slice
Ratafia biscuits	Almond cookies or Macaroons
Roast potatoes	Oven-browned potatoes
Scones	Biscuits
Self-raising flour	All-purpose self-rising flour
Single cream	Light cream
Soft brown sugar	Light brown sugar
Spring onion	Green onion
Stewing steak	Braising beef
Sultanas	Seedless white raisins
Treacle	Molasses
Wholemeal	Whole wheat

EQUIPMENT

British	American
Ashet	Meat dish
Baking sheet or tray	Cookie sheet
Frying pan	Skillet
Greaseproof paper	Waxed paper or aluminium foil
Stewpan or pan	Kettle
Large pot	Dutch Oven or deep-cooking utensil with a tight-fitting lid
Liquidiser	Electric blender
Roasting tin	Roasting pan with rack
Sandwich tins	Round-layer pans